ARTIFICIAL
INTELLIGENCE
FOR MANAGERS

INDIA · SINGAPORE · MALAYSIA

Notion Press

Old No. 38, New No. 6
McNichols Road, Chetpet
Chennai - 600 031

First Published by Notion Press 2020
Copyright © Rakesh Dandu 2020
All Rights Reserved.

ISBN 978-1-64892-642-6

ARTIFICIAL INTELLIGENCE FOR MANAGERS

For Individuals Aspiring to Get into the AI Domain

Includes 70+ Use Cases and 20+ Industries

RAKESH DANDU

INDIA • SINGAPORE • MALAYSIA

INDICACADEMY

INDIC PLEDGE

• *I celebrate our civilisational identity, continuity & legacy in thought, word and deed.*

• *I believe our indigenous thought has solutions for the global challenges of health, happiness, peace, and sustainability.*

• *I shall seek to preserve, protect and promote this heritage in doing so,*
    • *discover, nurture and harness my potential,*
    • *connect, cooperate and collaborate with fellow seekers,*
    • *be inclusive and respectful of diverse opinions.*

ABOUT INDIC ACADEMY

Indic Academy is a non-traditional 'university' for traditional knowledge. We seek to bring about a global renaissance based on Indic civilizational and indigenous thought. We are pursuing a multidimensional strategy across time, space and cause by establishing centers of excellence, transforming intellectuals and building an ecosystem.

Indic Academy is pleased to support this book.

dedicated to

my little princess, Diya.

Contents

Who This Book Is For?

"Well clearly, the final frontier has arrived."

The future is Artificial Intelligence (AI) and the sooner we as a society realize this, the more we will be able to appreciate and take advantage of this unprecedented situation within our own abilities.

However, many of us are either yet to make this decision, or simple unaware.

I started writing this book with an intention to specifically caters to those individuals who are intrigued by the idea of AI and are either hesitant or challenged on how to make that first move.

It is also for those who still are in dilemma as in where do they fit in the entire AI real, especially coming from a management or a non-technical executive background and provide them with a better understanding of where one stands in this topology. The book also provides certain guidance on how to quickly move forward in pursuit of a career in AI.

The book is non-technical in nature as much as it could be, clearly discussing the business impact of AI from an AI Product Manager's standpoint.

Hence, it is intended for all those who are currently employed in the capacity of HR Managers, Project Managers, Product Managers, Program Managers, any Management cadre, CXO's, Technical and Process trainers, Software Engineers, Developers, General Managers, HOS, Principals and all teachers including Computer Science . It is also for those who are enthusiastic about AI and wish to see themselves in an AI Product Management role in the future or just wishes to appreciate this technology.

The book "Artificial Intelligence for Managers" as an attempt, introduces non-technical managers and individuals to the world of Artificial Intelligence. Furthermore, it elaborates the imperatives for becoming an AI Product Managers by discussing various latest tools, frameworks and process of AI development.

Finally, I believe that this book will equip all the readers to contribute or at least, even start thinking towards the betterment of the socio-economic fabric surrounding us using AI.

> *"He will not let your foot slip—*
>
> *he who watches over you will not slumber"*

Psalm 121

Foreword

AI recently has moved quickly. Every day one can witness some profound changes being infused into our society and at the core of this one discovers the presence of AI. Clearly the undercurrents of something phenomenal can be felt. While many of us are acquainted with the developments in the field of applied AI, for most it is still an uncharted area.

Artificial intelligence (AI) for Managers" is a straightforward book that familiarizes one with this extremely technical subject. After reading through the book, you will appreciate that a new emerging life is finding its place around us and if not everything, most of the things that we know as of today will not only be touched by it but will also be governed by these AI systems no sooner than we think.

So, Should that frighten you?

No, not at all! In fact it should not and it will not if you intend to understand it. Secondary schooling and tertiary education curriculum already have AI as subjects but what about those who are in the mid of their careers and those who did not have this in their school or college syllabus. This book is precisely for them.

Rakesh has written this book keeping the managers in mind. These are those managers and individuals who have the responsibility to work and manage people. This is the segment which will be most impacted due to AI and hence the focus. The author does not leave you alone while you read the book. You will not find yourself reading it but you will find yourself listening to the author. The book skilfully takes you through various concepts within AI in a nutshell with ease and comfort.

From a beginner's question what AI is, to the applications of AI in different sectors, the author remains with you. Therefore, I strongly feel the book is significant for mangers for one reason that they are the agents of transformation in any organization. Rather than finding themselves outdated for not familiar with AI, managers including all resource administrators should update themselves with the knowledge of AI and maybe transform as human resource dealing with AI.

It can also be one of the easy books for leisure reading for those who may just want to understand AI as a layman. I recommend this book for everyone. This is a definite book for your libraries and training module of every organization and B-schools.

So, opening this book means opening a new window and enjoying the new sunshine.

Nirmesh Singh

Head of Public Affairs and Communications,

Construction Equipment Rental Association (CERA)

1. Introduction

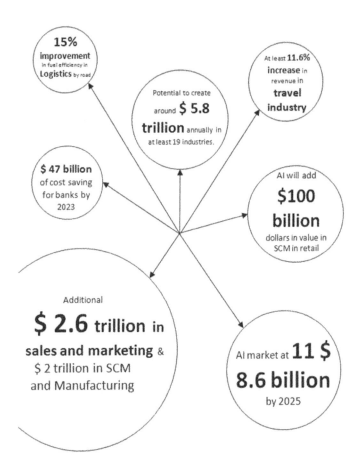

1.1 AI Market share

From the earliest days of computing, machines have incrementally outperformed humans at logical tasks such as solving simple math problems. However, other tasks like carrying on a conversation as a human interaction, identifying whether the animal in a picture is a dog or cat, or recognizing whether a person is happy or sad, have always been a challenge area for computers.

Although the term "*Artificial Intelligence*" was coined in the year 1956 by John Carthy, it is only recent that this term has actually taken the front seat and has garnered a lot of attention. This phenomena can be attributed to some of the long awaited breakthroughs in this field.

Due to various technological challenges in terms of both principles governing AI, coupled with non-existent computing power required to fuel this technology, the actual impetus to make this a real-life house-hold technology was clearly missing.

The phrase "Artificial Intelligence" was first used in reference to those tasks that are easy for humans and difficult for machines at the computer science workshop in USA.

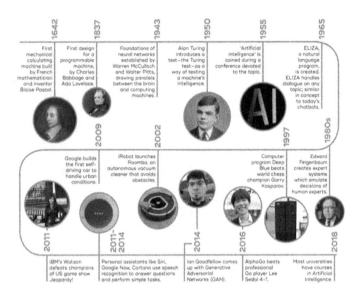

1.2 History of AI events

Courtesy: qbi.uq.edu.au

(The author does not retain any rights to the above image)

At the conclusion of the workshop, the attendees devoted themselves to figuring out "how to make machines use language, form abstractions and concepts, solve kinds of problems now reserved for humans, and improve themselves."

So, what is Artificial Intelligence? Well, simply put, a artificial intelligence is an ability to think the way a human thinks. It is the ability of the software to mimic human thinking capability.

To this day, AI researchers continue to work on the areas outlined by these early AI pioneers. Fields like natural language processing, image recognition and machine learning have become subspecialties within AI. Artificial intelligence research has also expanded to encompass other areas, such as social intelligence, creativity, autonomous vehicles, recommendation engines and much more.

According to a study, companies spent around $12.5 billion on cognitive and AI systems in 2017, a 59.3% more than they spent previous year. The market researchers now predict that the total revenue of such companies from AI cumulative will exceed by $46 billion by 2021. Clearly a lot of focus and plethora of opportunities to take advantage of.

2. AI Historical Events

The fascination of humans to create something similar to that of their own, goes to time in antiquity. Although AI took more measurable real-life manifestation in the 1700s, the seeds were sown in around 2700 BC with the invention of Abacus, when a device used to calculate numbers using beads was invented.

Jonathan Swift's novel "*Gulliver travels*" probably was the first text which mentioned the term "engine". The device or the engine as we know today, is capable of generating a certain set of results based upon certain input provided to it in a predefined environment.

Again the term "*Robots*" in Metropolis - a more recent play produced in 1927, for instance was the first which introduced an entity which was similar to humans and depict its impact on the society. In 1939, Atanasoff-Berry Computer (ABC) was developed to solve as many as twenty nine linear equations, simultaneously.

This was phenomenal and unprecedented as for the first time that such a feat was achieved in the history of automated computations.

"The Test setup has a Human Questioner,

a Human Respondent and Computer

Respondent."

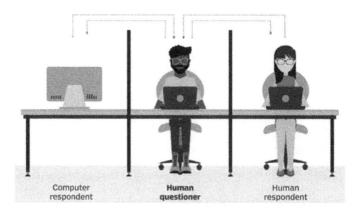

2.1 Turing Test Setup

By 1950s, it was a clear belief among scientists that machines shall have the ability to calculate, think at a certain level and capable to generate desired outputs.

Claude Shannon, recognized as the "the father of information theory", came up with an idea of a computer program which could replicate the skill of playing chess.

Similarly, Alan Turing, a mathematician, philosopher and a pioneer in the theoretical computer science & AI, was the first to succeed in solving various problems including the famous "*German Enigma code*". He was also the first to introduce "*the Turing test*".

Turing test has been the most profound experiment that could be conducted to evaluate a machine's ability to showcase an intelligent behavior similar to that of a human. Failing to do so indicated that the machine is not intelligent enough to be categorized as an AI machine.

By 1960s, industrial robots had been invented which were being used on assembly lines in General Motors. By now, checkers-playing, a self-learning game machine, and *LISP* (programming Language), which went on to become highly used AI development tool, were already introduced.

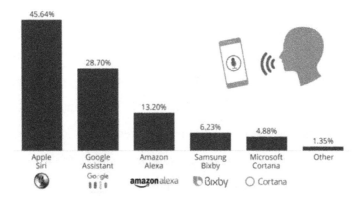

2.2 Recent study of US Market share in 2018

The decade also saw the introduction of concepts and programs like HAL (*Heuristically programmed Algorithmic Computer*), "first electronic person", and ELIZA, an interactive computer program (a chatbot) which today have become the foundation of many day-to-day AI business applications. People around the world had witnessed more of such advancements in the next ten years.

However, by 80's the steam had phased-out. This period is considered the "AI winter" due to the slowdown of investments in this field with an exception from the Japanese government, which allocated a huge sums of funds towards the development of fifth-generation computer projects in the field of *natural language processing* (NLP), *image processing* (IP), expression of humanlike reasoning (*Sentiments*).

Other, latest developments like *ASIMO*, an artificially intelligent humanoid robot, *Roomba*, an autonomous robot vacuum, NASA's robotic exploration, *ImageNet*, Google's driverless car, Kinect for *Xbox 360* - the first gaming device that tracked human body movement using a 3D camera and infrared detection, *IBM's watson*, *Apple's Siri*, a virtual assistant on *Apple iOS*, *Microsoft's Cortana*, and finally *Amazon's Alexa* have taken machine capability into the next big leap.

But, this is not all. One of the most profound AI programs in recent times has been Google's *AlphaGo* introduced in 2015, a board game which has already defeated many humans. Similarly, "*Sofia*" created by Hanson Robotics is known to be the "*first robot citizen*". Her ability to make various facial expressions and recognizing the same makes her a "truly AI robot".

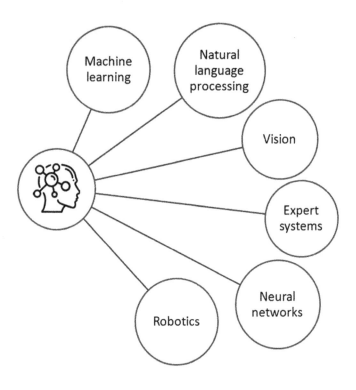

2.3 Areas of AI

Some of the most recent inventions in the field of AI starting in 2016 has been the "*Personal Assistant*" by Google. The introduction of advanced "*chatbots*" also called as "the dialogue agents" by Facebook in 2017 that has the ability to converse with other humans flawlessly, now, also has a knack to negotiate.

Currently, a huge number of inventions are being done in the field of speech recognition, AI optimized hardware (*GPU* accelerated hardware), cyber defense, robotics, content creation and more.

With endless new use cases of AI implementation emerging every day, it is only a matter of time that the rudimentary functions of our daily life will be replaced by more optimized and cost-effective AI solutions.

3. Terms to Know

Now, before we move further, it would be wise-enough to go through some of the terms and AI vocabulary.

Algorithm

The dictionary definition for an algorithm is "a process or set of rules to be followed in calculations or other problem-solving operations, especially by a computer." In layman terms, when we are talking about algorithms, we are talking about processes, usually processes related to mathematics.

When you were in third or fourth grade, you learned the algorithm for long division. You learned a process that involved dividing, multiplying, subtracting and bringing down to the next digit.

When we talk about algorithms for AI and machine learning, we're talking about similar kind of processes — just a lot more elaborate. For example, Google uses an algorithm (a process based on rules) to determine which websites appear at the top of its search results. In machine learning, systems use many different types of algorithms in order to achieve desired results. Common examples include decision trees, clustering algorithms, classification algorithms or regression algorithms. We Will see the definition soon.

Artificial general intelligence (AGI):

This is also known as strong AI, AGI is a type of artificial intelligence that is considered human-like, and still in its preliminary stages (more of a hypothetical existence in present day).

Artificial neural network (ANN):

A network modeled after the human brain by creating an artificial neural system usually via a pattern-recognizing computer algorithm that learns from, interprets, and classifies sensory data.

Back propagation:

A short for "backward propagation of errors," is a method of training neural networks where the system's initial output is compared to the desired output, then adjusted until the difference (between outputs) becomes minimal.

Bayesian networks:

Also known as Bayes network consists of Bayes model, belief network, and decision network. It is a graph-based model representing a set of variables and their dependencies. It is a network model to determine the probability of a condition.

Big data:

large amounts of structured and unstructured data that is too complex to be handled by standard data-processing software.

Chatbots:

A chat robot is a software that can converse with a human user through text or voice commands. It is being utilized by e-commerce, education, health, and business industries for a seamless communication interface and to answer user questions.

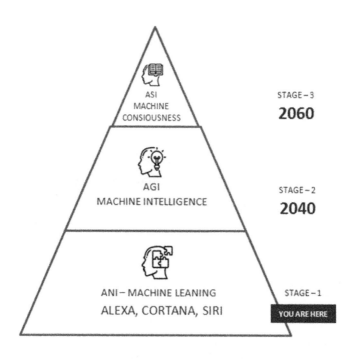

3.1 AI Development Timeline

Classification:

It is an algorithm technique that allows machines to assign categories to data points.

Clustering:

An algorithm technique that allows machines to group similar data into larger data categories.

Cognitive computing:

This is a computerized model that mimics human thought processes by data mining, Natural Language Processing (NLP), and pattern recognition. This is another name given to AI.

Data mining:

The process of sorting through large sets of data in order to identify recurring patterns while establishing problem-solving relationships. Data mining is all about looking for patterns in a set of data. It identifies correlations and trends that might otherwise go unnoticed. For example, if a data mining application were given Walmart's sales data, it might discover that people in the South prefer certain brands of chips or that during the month of October people will buy anything with "Soya" in the product name.

Data mining tools don't necessarily have to include machine learning or deep learning capabilities, but today's most advanced data mining software generally does have these features built-in.

Deep learning:

Deep Learning a machine learning technique that teaches computers how to learn by rote method (i.e. machines mimic learning as a human mind would, by using classification techniques).

Just like machine learning is a subset of artificial intelligence. Deep learning is a subset of machine learning. It is a part of machine learning that focuses on forming "abstractions and concepts." Deep learning systems ingest large quantities of data and generalize categories and features related to that data through supervised or unsupervised learning.

TRADITIONAL MACHINE LEARNING

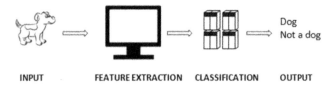

| INPUT | FEATURE EXTRACTION | CLASSIFICATION | OUTPUT |

DEEP LEARNING

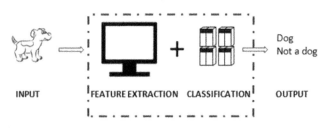

3.2 Traditional vs Deep Learning ML Models

To understand how this works, consider the problem of teaching a computer to distinguish pictures of cats from pictures of dogs. Programmers could try to come up with a set of rules that explains exactly what a cat is and exactly what a dog is, but even though humans can easily distinguish a cat from a dog, it's really hard to explain that difference using algorithms that a computer can understand.

However, a deep learning system can analyze a whole bunch of pictures of animals and come to its own generalizations about what distinguishes a cat from a dog. While the cat-dog example is pretty innocuous, this type of deep learning can also be very controversial, such as the deep learning system that learned to distinguish whether people were gay or straight by looking at pictures of their faces. Deep learning systems rely on neural networks which will be discussed further.

GPU:

Short for "graphical processing unit," a GPU is a computer chip that is especially good at processing lots of data in a parallel processing mode. They were originally designed to handle video and graphics (hence the name), but they are also excellent at big data processing and machine learning tasks.

Supervised and unsupervised:

Within machine learning and deep learning, there are several possible approaches to teaching computers. Two of the most common once are supervised and unsupervised learning.

With supervised learning, the computer has a "teacher," a human being (or several human beings) that provides examples. In the cat-dog identification example, we have been using. Supervised learning would require a person to label a bunch of pictures as either cats or dogs. The computer would then learn from those sample inputs and outputs.

In unsupervised learning, the computer doesn't have any sample data. Instead, the system is asked to find patterns in the data on its own. This technique is useful when looking for hidden insights in big data.

Other common types of machine learning include semi-structured learning, where the system gets partial sample data sets.

Reinforcement learning

This is another form of learning where in the system learns through its environment by interacting with it and then by getting rewards or punishments based on how well it completes an assigned tasks.

Genetic algorithm:

Interestingly, this is an algorithm based on principles of genetics that is used to efficiently and quickly find solutions to difficult biotic or genetic problems.

Heuristic:

As the name suggests, it is a computer science technique designed for quick, optimal, solution-based problem solving in a self discovery mode.

Image recognition:

the process of identifying or detecting an object or feature of an object in an image or video.

Machine learning (ML):

ML is a subset of the larger artificial intelligence category. Going back to the proposal from that first artificial intelligence workshop, machine learning is the part of artificial intelligence that focuses on giving computers the ability to "improve themselves" over a period of time as a result of experience. An early computer scientist named Arthur Samuel explained that machine learning enables computers "to learn without being explicitly programmed".

Computer scientists have come up with a lot of different ways to help computers learn. For example, they might use supervised or unsupervised learning algorithms to help machines get better at performing tasks over time. Today, As more cases are exposed to them, they get better every day. We encounter machine learning every time we see a recommendation engine like the one at Amazon or Netflix that suggest products we might like to buy or movies we might like to watch. Machine learning has also become an important part of big data analytics tools used by enterprises today.

Neural Networks:

Neural networks go by lots of different names: artificial neural network, neural net, deep neural net and other similar terms. All those phrases describe a similar thing — a computer system inspired by "*living brains*".

In the workshop held in 1956 at Hampshire, United States, where scientists first discussed artificial intelligence at length, the attendees thought that "*every aspect of learning or any other feature of intelligence can in principle be so precisely described that a machine can be made to simulate it*". In fact, they thought it would be so easy to create a machine model of a human brain that it would take ten scientists just two months to accomplish it.

However, that timeline was more than a little unrealistic, considering that researchers are still working on creating computer brains that function like human brains.

Nevertheless, over the years, computer scientists have made a lot of progress toward that goal.

Today, neural networks, using nodes that are roughly analogous to biological neurons, perform many tasks related to computer vision, speech recognition, board game strategy and more.

Natural language processing (NLP):

Computers have always been able to understand programming languages, but understanding regular English or Chinese or any other vernacular is much more complicated.

Natural language processing is an area of artificial intelligence related to understanding and generating speech the way humans usually use it. It helps computers process, interpret, and analyze human language and its characteristics by using natural language data.

You have probably experienced the evolution of natural language processing with your own use of search engines. In the early days of the Internet, users typed Boolean operators to help them search for keywords. So, if you were looking for some data online, you might have typed 'artificial intelligence' OR *'machine learning'* AND 'terms'" into the search engine and the engine would have searched it's "database" and showed you some results.

But, search engines have much better natural language processing capabilities, so you can just type "What is artificial intelligence?" to get a definition, as well as links to resources.

Optical Character Recognition (OCR):

conversion of images of text (typed, handwritten, or printed) either electronically or mechanically, into machine-encoded text is what OCR is about.

Predictive Analytics:

Today, nearly all companies are running analytics on their big data. Predictive analytics is a particular type of analytics that seeks to tell users what's going to happen next in simple words "foretell". For example, you might feed a predictive analytics system ten years of sales data from your company and then ask it to forecast your sales for next quarter given the current trends.

Today's predictive analytics systems usually incorporate data mining and machine learning capabilities, and often can be viewed as a step toward artificial intelligence. They rely on algorithms to help them process data and determine likely future events.

Reinforcement learning:

A machine learning method where the reinforcement algorithm learns by interacting with its environment, and is then penalized or rewarded based on the decisions it makes.

Robotic process automation (RPA):

RPA uses software with artificial intelligence and machine learning capabilities to perform repetitive tasks once completed by humans. These are primarily used in industrial production lines or assemblies.

Turing Test:

This is a test created by computer scientist *Alan Turing* (1950) to see if machines could exhibit intelligence equal to or indistinguishable from that of a human.

The *Turing Test* named after its inventor, was an early computer scientist who theorized extensively about artificial intelligence. He proposed a simple test to determine whether or not a computer had achieved true artificial intelligence. A human interrogator would type questions, which would then be given to a computer system and a human being. The computer and the human being would then type responses. If the interrogator cannot tell which response came from the computer and which came from the person, the system would, in Turing's opinion, have attained artificial intelligence.

In recent years, several AI systems have been said to have passed the Turing Test, but the results have always been somewhat controversial. Some people question whether the Turing Test is really a good way to evaluate artificial intelligence, but it remains influential in discussions about AI.

4. AI Project Roles

So now that we have certain understanding of AI, it is equally important to know where one can fit into this universe.

AI Product Manager (AI-PM)

AI product vision development works closely with the users to define the product specifications. This is done with thorough analysis of the requirement and laying down a priority for the same. Essentially, AI-PM is an individual who has deep understanding of both the product development process as well as the knack to bring the entire Product Development team including stake holders onto one plane and then finally ensuring the delivery of the final product. Additional skills including technical are highly desirable as then one may also take additional responsibilities of a system architect as well. Further, this would help them support the process of defining the technical specifications for the product as well.

Data Scientist

Data Scientist primarily perform Statistical Analysis. A Data Scientist is someone who creates value out of existing data or datasets. A data scientist generally has the following skills:

They work with algorithm design and analysis such as *Linear algebra, Probability Mathematical Concept and Statistics*. They also use scripting and modeling language and tools like such as *Python* and *MATLAB*. They are also expected to work on data management language such as *SQL*, and *MongoDB*, and relational databases like *MySQL*

Conceptually, a data scientist is one who is capable of working on any of the AI-based product development projects. Depending upon the industry specific experience and field of interest, one can choose a domain to work in.

Data Engineer

Primarily, this is an AI Engineering role. This role requires the models to be implemented through scripts as "*Software Programs*". A data engineer role is to build machine learning algorithms to work on large data (sets).

AI DEVELOPMENT ROLES

TRADITIONAL ROLES

Analyst	Scrum	UX Designers	Front End Developer	Product Manager	Quality Analyst	Back End Developer

Data Scientists

4.1 Role of Data Scientist in AI

Required skills may include:

- Analyzing and Designing Mathematical Algorithms

- Using scripting and modeling language and tools such as Python and MATLAB

- Classification, Regression, or Clustering models

- Knowledge of frameworks (Spark, H2O.ai)

- A data management language such as SQL, and MongoDB, and relational databases like MySQL and Oracle

- Version control such as Github

- Managing Cloud computing (for example, Amazon Web Services, Microsoft Azure, or Google Cloud)

Development Operations (DevOps) Engineer

This role is expected to maintain the infrastructure of a project and hence needs solid software engineering skills, knowledge of operating systems, *distributed systems*, and *cloud computing*.

Required skills may include:

- AI Algorithm design and analysis

- API Architecture, design and deployment

- Database/Backend (SQL, PostgreSQL, MySQL, Oracle) along with a scripting language

- Cloud computing such as, Amazon Web Services, Microsoft Azure, or Google Cloud)

- Continuous deployment platform such as Travis C1 which has a support for other existing platforms.

- Distributed systems and NoSQL databases such as Hadoop, Cassandra, HBase, Kafka, Dynamo, Redis, MongoDB, or ElasticSearch

- Enterprise version control such as Bitbucket

Software Engineer (Back End)

Software Engineers (Backend) would develop APIs, configure databases and write business logics for various business applications including carts, payment gateways, authentications, notifications, and so on. Some of the popular technologies they should be proficient would be *Node.js, Flask, Django, Ruby on Rails, Akka, Spray, PostgreSQL, MySQL, MongoDB, Redis, and RabbitMQ.*

Software Engineer (Web Front End, Mobile)

Primarily, a Front End developer who builds user interfaces for web applications. Skill set for this may include *React.js, Angular.js, D3.js, Vue.js, Node.js, HTML, JavaScript, CSS, Bower, Gulp, Less, Bootstrap, and jQuery.*

Full Stack Developer (MERN, MEAN)

Full stack developers are considered as technical individuals with experience in developing all fronts (Stacks) of technology i.e backend, frontend and the business rules. Companies prefer to have either MEAN (*MongoDB, Express.js, AngularJS and Node.js*) or MERN (*MongoDB, Express.js, React.js and Node.js*) stack developers.

Designer (User experience)

Essentially develops graphic design/interfaces based upon the user experience use cases. Typically, creates an initial prototype, collaborates with the product manager to test it with the users, and prepares the final front-end code which can be integrated by the engineer. Tools may include *Adobe Photoshop*, *Sketch*, and *InVision*. These designs can be for both Mobile interfaces as well as for the website.

Project Manager

The captain of the ship, responsible for the overall development of the project ensuring overall team coordination, task planning and scheduling, aligning resources for the tasks and ensuring the project deadlines are met as per the technical specifications and within the commercial constraint.

System/Technical Architect

A highly technically skilled senior person with relevant project execution and delivery experience who can converts product specifications into engineering components. Component level planning and design and the integration of these components at various software layers. This includes designing and developing APIs, stubs, dependencies and so on.

Product Quality Assurance Analyst

Ensures that the product meets the specified features and that the software works flawlessly as per pre-defined product requirements. They may also contribute in checking out from an machine learning model and undertake output analysis along with the AI team members.

5. Underlying Process Models

AI uses various mathematical and statistical models to make decisions. Since this could be extremely heavy on processing, the models are designed in such a way so as to improve upon the productivity and scalability of the solution so developed. As mentioned earlier, these models mimic the neurons in our brain and hence "Artificial Intelligence".

From the implementation point of view, multiple layers of such AI networks are used to ascertain a solution or answer. As product manager, it would be advantageous to know more about these underlying models as mentioned below to form a grip on the topic:

Process Models

- *Linear regression*

- *Logistic Regression*

- *Decision Tree*

- *Naive Bayes*

- *K Nearest Neighbors*

- *Bayesian*

- *Learning Vector Quantization*

- *Neural Network algorithms like SVM* (Support Vector Machines)

AI underlying process models

Talking about models, these are basically algorithms that run behind-the-scenes for the AI to perform. Now depending upon the industry use cases change. And with every use case the expectation from the underlying algorithm to perform also changes, and hence various models have been developed in recent past. Further, this process is continued even today as this book is being written.

Supervised learning

This process of AI learning requires human intervention to teach computers how to classify objects or data based on features we specify. In this, Classification and Regression are two most popular methods used for supervised learning. Algorithms under these include *Decision Tree, Naive Bayes, Linear Regression and SVM* (Supervised Vector Machines).

Unsupervised learning

Since in unsupervised learning there is no predetermined result being expected, the only thing we do is to just provide huge amounts of data and let the model figure out features and other classification criteria for instance size, color and shape. Two types of unsupervised learning are Clustering and Association. General algorithms being used under this includes *K-means, hierarchical, Apriori and Genetic.*

Reinforcement learning

As the name suggests, the entire idea behind this is to maximize the rewards for positive actions and punishing for unwarranted once. In other words, learning by putting the best behavior forward to earn maximum points. This is quite similar to the way we humans prefer to teach small children. They are rewarded for their good deeds while punished for making mistakes. This mechanism motivates a child to perform better next time.

Let us look at some of the popular models that are being used in various aspects of AI projects.

Linear regression

Linear regression is a part of mathematical statistics, and has been around for over two centuries now. Represented as

Y= a + bX,

where Y is dependent upon X.

It is a mathematical model to help understand the dependency and relationship between two different variables related to each other in a certain equation. In other words, this also means identifying the relation (regression) between two variables, one dependent and the other independent.

Logistic regression

Also known as *Logit Regression*, is used to guess the probability of an occurrence of an event with respect to certain data provided. As the name suggests the model works in a binary fashion such as *win/lose, gain/loss, on-off, go/no-go.*

Decision trees

One of the most efficient and the oldest model known and used. It is a tree shaped model with leaves or nodes as *"yes" or "no"*. Every node of this tree is a decision tree where it needs to decide upon a condition at every level. Depending on the leaf chosen, the control moves to the next node.

Naive Bayes

It is a model used to solve some of the most complex problems. Typically this is a classifier model which acts as a bundle or "collection" of various algorithms also known as "family of algorithms". Using this method one can predict, the degree of dependence between various features. This helps in further short listing and preferring one feature over other.

K-nearest neighbors (KNN)

While this is the most basic of the models, it is also one of the most powerful ones. It uses a *non-parametric technique* (no assumptions being made) which is used for conducting regression and classification of data. In this, some prior training data is already provided which helps in classifying groups based on certain tree identified attributes.

Support Vector Machine

Basically this is an extension of support vector classifier which is used for the generalization to support *non-linear class boundaries*. For now, clearly this sounds very technical and definitely needs more understanding. But to clarify this to some more extent, imagine a scenario where one needs to classify a group of people into obese and non-obese.

One clear way would be to get an average difference weights in weights of both the groups and then anyone falling within that weight group would be classified as obese or maybe not. However, what happens when someone is just outside the margin of obese. Should the person be considered as obese or not? This is the classic scenario where SVM comes to help.

Hierarchical clustering

Known as *Hierarchical cluster analysis* (HCA), is a technique whereby similar clusters are grouped together within a decision tree structure with a bottom-up approach.

Apriori

It is basically an algorithm driven by database, which is useful in analyzing data and underlying business rules. One remarkable implementation of this algorithm could be to recommend relevant products to the customers automatically.

Genetic Algorithm

This is an abstraction of human genetics proposed by *John Holland.* It is an algorithm inclined towards *heuristic study* reflecting natural selection by various biological processes. It is set of procedures to find the optimized technique for developing the next generation.

6. Types of AI

Artificial Intelligence exists in three different types

- *Artificial Narrow Intelligence (ANI)*

- *Artificial General Intelligence (AGI)*

- *Artificial Super Intelligence* (ASI) the best and the most challenging one to implement for now.

1. Artificial Narrow Intelligence (ANI)

It is one of the streams of AI which is proficient in performing a single task. The idea is that the AI program learns to tackle a single problem inherently i.e intelligently by studying the test data and developing inferences. It is considered to be at level I.

Few Examples

Speech Recognition, is one such example wherein the model can recognize speech. Voice Assistants such as *Cortana*, *Alexa* which responds through voice commands also fall under this category.

2. Artificial General Intelligence (AGI)

As the name suggests, it is a general-purpose intelligence in nature. It also means that it reflects an intellect similar to that of a human brain.

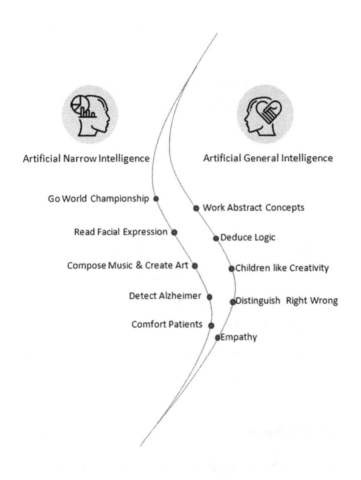

6.1 ANI VS AGI

This ability makes it possible for AGI to learn and improve its own cognition through various learning methods.

AlphaGo, for instance in a way can be categorized as an AGI. Although it only plays the game for now, its intelligence can be replicated and applied to various other domains. Since a lot of work is being done in AGI, we are yet to achieve the full scale of humanlike possibilities.

3. Artificial Super Intelligence (ASI)

Artificial Super is assumed to be an intelligence which is far more superior than what humans have today. This intelligence surpasses the human intellect in terms of every single activity that we do and know of today including reading, writing and dealing with abstract topics. Also given the fact that a human brain has few billion neurons, would act as a deterrent to words higher levels of cognition.

Neural Networks

A neural network consists of many processors within it. Although these processors work simultaneously, they are arranged in a certain layered manner called as tiers. Hence every tier has a specific role to play. The responsibility of the tier is to receive certain input from the previous layer and provide an output to the next layer.

So, the first tier for instance receives the raw natural input say an image of our flower through the eye optic nerves. This data is then forwarded to the next layer to extract various features until it reaches the last layer giving out the final result. Hence each layer plays a unique role in analyzing the input.

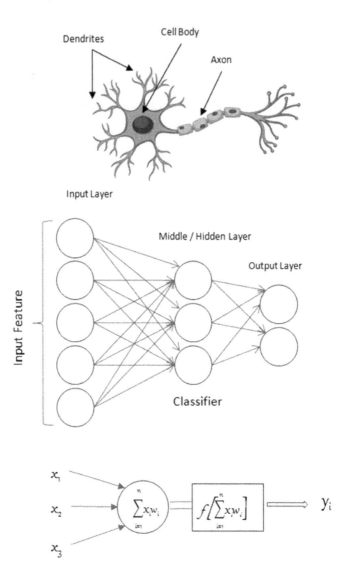

6.1 Comparison of Neural and Deep Neural Networks

At the start and the end of these tiers are information hold areas also called as *nodes* . These nodes are connected before and after each tier. It is in these nodes that various information such as rules and self learnt knowledge are stored. These nodes are also responsible to allocate highest importance or weights to those inputs which heavily impact the result towards forming an output.

Deep Learning Neural Network

Deep learning is a specialized field of machine learning. It is a natural technique to teach computers just as we humans learn which is through "*Exemplification*". Sound implementations of Deep learning includes automated driving, auto coloring of old black-and-white pictures and movies, language learning and so on.

Deep learning network algorithms do not need a human intervention to teach them what to do with the input. It acts much like a human brain, naturally analyzing what is coming in and intelligently updating its own knowledgebase. It does so by "*classifying*" objects in various forms and means. Just like the "*Classification model*", there exists other such models which facilitate AI deep learning to perform tasks exceedingly challenging similar to human intelligence and much more. These networks include *Convolution model* and *Recurrent model* under Supervised learning. So Deep learning models need large sets of labeled data to get trained.

7. Project Lifecycle

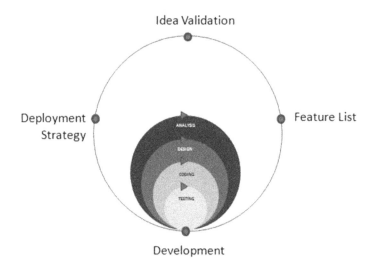

7.1 AI -Product Software Development

Before we move to the AI product Lifecycle, it is only logical to stress upon the Software product life cycle.

Software product development is indeed a challenging area that requires both deep technical knowledge and expertise as well as long-term commitment and vision to succeed. Although there is a common misconception that programming is the only thing important in the process of software development, clearly it is not the fact. Let's look at various stages of software product engineering life-cycle.

Software Product Development Phases

1. Requirements identification: Idea Validation and Product Definition:
This should be the first step towards an effective product requirements gathering from the customers of the client.

This process is an exercise to understand if the product idea is even viable or not by giving a clear definition of the product itself from the feedback of the customers. Questions like What is the product about, Who would be the end user of the product, USP of the product and so on.

7.2 Machine Learning Development Lifecycle

Since this is the first process where requirements are being evaluated, it requires a thorough discussion on some of the questions mentioned above to draw a right inferences towards a successful product development.

2. Product Prototype development: Features

Once the need of the customer with respect to the product is understood, a clear definition of what is known as the "exhaustive feature list" is generated. At this point the actual users of the product must be taken into account to maximize their *User Experience*(UX). Also the participation of *subject matter experts* (SME) should be taken into consideration, especially for domain based product development.

3. Product Minimal Viable Product Development (MVP) stage:

This is the most preferred step undertaken by product managers. As the name suggests, a minimalistic featured product is designed before a full-fledged product development is taken up. This also helps those companies which are looking for investors to invest into their ideas rather than developing a complete product and then going into the market. This forms the first version of the product which acts as a baseline against certain features. From the standard waterfall structure this is one phase where the software development process differs as it implements an iterative process of development. Nowadays, Agile methodology is being heavily implemented within organizations.

4. Other considerations:

Further based upon this, Project Management Lifecycle (*Analysis, Design, Development, Testing*), use of Technologies and Architecture Design are taken into consideration.

Since there are a lot of software tools available in the market, choosing the correct product architecture and technology can truly make or break a product in the future. As a product manager, one should be aware of all these factors from a customer standpoint and ensure that the product development is both flexible to change to most part of it and scalable.

5. Product Deployment Strategies:

As a *product manager*, one should consider various product deployment options to best reach the end customer, the last mile. Ideally off-the-shelf solution are best suited for this task since it is the customers who should be able to manage the product installations on their own without any external assistance. *Mobile solutions* for instance, demand a hassle-free installation process by the customers.

6. Product Marketing Plan:

Product marketing plan is an integral part of an effective software product development. *Distribution network, partnerships,* and other means should be a part of the marketing plan depending on the target audience of the product.

8. AI Product Development Lifecycle

Unlike the software development process, interestingly AI product development process is extensively iterative in nature at the core. Hence, you would only declare the current cycle of production as "complete" until you have reached the desired benchmark, before moving to the next iteration.

Task Planning and AI Project Setup Phase: So before the AI-ML project is initiated, following are the aims of this phase

- To define the scope of requirements
- To assess project feasibility
- To define general model tradeoffs (accuracy vs speed)
- Data collection and labeling (Training Data)
- To collect right set of data for both testing and training
- Cleansing and appropriation
- Validating the data so collected
- Going back to step one to ensure data is sufficient for desired benchmark

The next step is to work on AI-Model. Some of the crucial steps undertake in this phase include:

AI Model Assessment

- Baselining model performance and accuracy (since there are many models available)

- Prototyping AI model using data collected in step two

- Model fitment on training data (calibration process)

- Parallel experimentation on various ideas during early stages

- Search for state-of-the-art model for the problem (if available) and reproduce results and apply them to your dataset as a second benchmark

- Now go back to Step 1 and ensure enhanced scope feasibility

- Revisit Step 2 and ensure both quality and quantity is sufficient

Model Refinement Phase

- Undertake Model-performance parameter optimization also called as "hyperparameter" tuning

- Keep debugging the model repeatedly as more features are added as "*complexity*"

- Study the most common failure cases an optimize the model

- Refine data by going back to step two

Testing and Evaluation

- Evaluate the model test data distribution in terms of "*trained*" *versus* "*untrained*"

- Revisit hyperparameters

- Design tests cases:

- As per input data

- Model functionality

- Specific scenarios

Deployment Phase

- Expose model as a web-based offering such as *REST - API*

- Initially deploy the new model as *"Beta" version* to small set of users before rolling out to the public as *"Production"*

- Ensure code maintenance through version control

- Ongoing model maintenance

- keep track of any new changes in the data as this may affect the model adversely

- provision to retrain model periodically/as the case may be

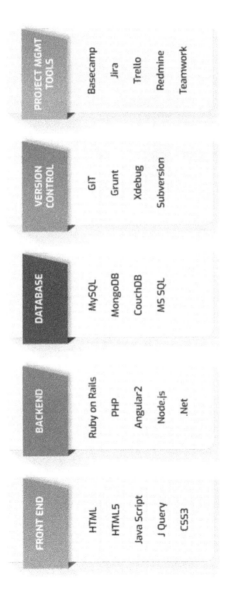

8.1 popular software list

Components of AI Software Development

Full Stack Development

Full stack development is a process of building a software end-to-end. This means that developing all the components right from the front-end to interface with the user, the middle tier to process the data, back-end to store the data, and finally integrating with tools such as Amazon Web Server) *AWS - infrastructure management.* Nowadays, this has become a trend to hire Full Stack Developers.

These are resources who are experts in working with all the latest software development tier technologies, though many believe that a true full stack developer does not exist as it requires a lot of technical expertise and experience which is hard to find.

8.2 Front-end technologies

8.3 Back-end technologies

9. AI Libraries & Frameworks

Commercial and Academic

Before we move on to the Framework, let us look at some of the most popular and widely used AI Libraries.

AI Libraries

Pytorch (Python Library)

Pytorch is the Python implementation of Torch framework. It is an ML library initially developed by Facebook. PyTorch primarily is used for computer vision applications as well as natural language processing (NLP) as it provides dynamic computational graphs in a Recurrent Neural Network (RNN) model. It is one of the most preferred libraries among ML users as it makes complex architectures to be built upon conveniently.

Pros and Cons:

(+) Lots of software modules, easy to integrate custom layer types and executes on GPU

(+) huge range of pre-trained models available

(-) No commercial support as it is an open source

TensorFlow (Python Library)

Initially created by Google to replace Theano which was developed by Montreal Institute for Learning Algorithms (MILA). It is a complete end-to-end ML platform. So if you are willing to get some hands-on in ML, this is where you may start.

Pros and Cons

(+) Python implementation of Numpy library (a large collection of high-level mathematical functions)

(+) Computational graph abstraction, similar to Theano

(+) Faster compilation than Theano

(+) Inbuilt TensorBoard (dashboard) for ML metric visualization

(+) Support for Data and model Parallelism

(-) Slower and less user-friendly than other frameworks like Keras

(-) Much bulkier than Torch; as it has both high-level and low-level APIs

(-) Limited pre-trained models available

(-) No commercial support

CNTK

CNTK or "Computational Network Toolkit" is Microsoft's open-source deep-learning framework. The library includes feed-forward DNNs, convolutional nets and recurrent networks. CNTK offers a Python API over C++ code. It has not adopted any standard hence, not licensed for commercial use.

DSSTNE (Deep Scalable Sparse Tensor Network Engine)

Amazon like others, has its own set of libraries and APIs for both machine learning and deep learning. DSSTNE, although was released after Tensorflow and CNTK, no backup from Amazon for its use with AWS is available, clearly there seems to be no future for this. It is largely coded in C++, DSSTNE appears to be fast, although it has not attracted as large a community as the other libraries have.

Keras (Python Library)

Keras is one of the best Python libraries for deep-learning leaving behind TensorFlow, CNTK and Theano and can run on top of them. Hence, it acts as a wrapper for these.

(+) It is an Intuitive API

(+) It has a strong foothold among the existing frameworks

(+) Assumed standard for Python API for Neural Networks

LightGBM (Python Library)

Gradient Boosting Machine is a tree based learning algorithm and one of the most popular machine learning library for developing new elementary models and decision trees. It has both fast and efficient method of implementation. It has a support for both parallel and GPU based learning and can handle large-scale data.

Scikit

Scikit-learn was initially developed as a Google's project in 2007. Scikit-learn provides algorithms for both supervised and unsupervised learning through a standard interface in Python.

This stack that includes:

- NumPy: Base n-dimensional array package
- Matplotlib: Comprehensive 2D/3D plotting
- SciPy: Fundamental library for scientific computing
- IPython: Enhanced interactive console
- Pandas: Data structures and analysis

- Sympy: Symbolic mathematics

SystemML

SystemML is IBM's machine-learning framework, performs various AI tasks including Descriptive Statistics, Classification, Clustering, Regression, Matrix Factorization and Survival Analysis. It also has support for vector machines. However, SystemML development need additional deep-learning GPU capabilities such as importing and running neural network architectures and pre-trained models for training. Hence, it cannot independently sustain the AI development process.

Some Popular Computer Vision Frameworks

OpenCV -learn

OpenCV (Open Source Computer Vision Library) is an open source computer vision and machine learning software library with more than 2500 optimized algorithms, along with an exhaustive set of both classic and State-of-the-art (SoTA) computer vision (CV) and ML algorithms. OpenCV algorithms capabilities include detection and faces recognition, objects identification and tracking, human action and moments detection in videos, camera movement tracking, 3D model extraction, images/seen stitching, image search, red eyes removal, video processing watermarking and overlays and etc. It has extensive support for C++, Python, Java and MATLAB interfaces on Windows, Linux, Android and Mac OS. OpenCV is best suited for real-time vision applications.

Point Cloud Library

The Point Cloud Library (or PCL) is yet another library which supports large scale 2D/3D image & point cloud processing. It contains of numerous SoTA which includes filtering, feature estimation, surface reconstruction, segmentation and more.

ROS (Robot Operating System)

ROS is an open source framework used for the development of robotics including navigation. It takes inputs from various sources for decision-making. So, for any kind of requirement for robot development, ROS is the key.

MATLAB

MATLAB is a high-performance proprietary programming language as mathematically expressed notational computing. Hence, there are a lot mathematical symbols used in programming to produce various graphic elements including charts and graphs. It allows the developers to work with matrix, mapped function plotting and etc. It is also extensively used for data analytics, deep learning algorithms, computer vision, signal processing, and more.

CUDA (Compute Unified Device Architecture)

CUDA graphics processing units or GPUs are specialized set of hardware for processing images and complex calculations of huge data sets. As GPUs are being excessively applied to AI acceleration, GPU manufacturers have embedded NN (neural network) support into the hardware itself to accelerate these tasks.

POPULAR SPEECH (NLP FRAMEWORKS)

spaCy

spaCy is a free, open-source library for advanced Natural Language Processing (NLP) in Python and is used for commercial purpose. Developers can now build applications that process large volumes of text based data. They can also build "information extraction for *deep learning based*" applications such as sentiment extraction using spaCy.

Gensim

Another SoTA NLP text processing package is "Gensim" that does 'Topic Modeling for Humans' using vector models such as Word2Vec, FastText etc.

10. The Maverick

Product Manager - Tools & Competencies

Core Competencies for AI Product Manager

Being at the epi-centre of product development, there are various skills an AI product manager is expected to possess. While some of these could be a result of the academic background, most of these skills comes from varied and extensive work or project exposure. Some examples of these competencies may include:

- to study market demand with an ability to conduct customer interview sessions and product testing skills

- ability to undertake product design iteration

- knack for product feature identification and prioritization as per business need and subsequent planning of product rollout

- smooth translating business expectations into technical requirements

- revenue, pricing modeling

- product license distribution strategy

- and finally the ability to define and track product success metrics

10.1 Product Manager

However, all the above-mentioned can be prioritized into the following:

Product Design experience

When we say product design, a lot comes from what is known as "market needs" or the "customer requirements". Hence, as a product manager, one needs to be open to collect feedback for requirements before the product design process is initiated. At the same time, a product manager must have certain domain experience or enough exposure to accommodate ideas which could enhance the overall user experience (UX). Hence, while designing, one should be careful about user context, their background, and their expectations.

One may start from drawing raw sketches and general ideation and this should manifest into the "smallest details viable ".

For instance, one may ask questions like:

- How to identify spam messages and automatically remove them from inbox?

- How would you improve school search?

Analytical bent of mind

AI product managers should be good with numbers. They should be able to identify and define right metrics for product performance. Hence, they should be able to take decisions based on the analysis of the results they get from various product tests. They should be hands-on with such analysis. Skills may include writing SQL queries; working with testing scripts, analyzing data on Excel sheets and so on.

For instance, some of the interesting questions could be:

- How many API hits can an AWS server with X configuration can it serve?

- How many iPhones users are active between 10 and 11 every Sunday in Asia?

Technical skills

Needless to say, technical skills adds definite advantage in managing AI-based products. A decent exposure in AI technology that we have already discussed in a previous chapters would enable the candidate to lead successfully in this field. Therefore, understanding various models and frameworks from the point of their pros and cons could be extremely helpful.

For instance, *"which is a better model Tensorflow vs Keras and why?"*

Devising Strategy

Personally, I think this is one skill that weighs far more than others. While an AI product manager will be assessed by various product roles like technical and non-technical, it is the management skill which is most important when it comes to deciding both the product development path as well as the "go to market" strategy. For this reason, the acumen for product packaging from a feature point of view, and the quickness of the mind for taking instant decisions is primal.

For instance "Should we wait for the next big launch or should we go for two sub-version product launches?" could be an interesting question to solve.

AI Project Management Tools

So let's discuss some of the most popular products available for AI Managers to manage their projects better. These are the tools that help ease the job by providing collaboration and project monitoring.

Jira

I think this should be the first management tool to be talked about. Although you need to pay for the subscription, there is always a free one available.

Primarily, it is an issue tracking software which utilizes agile methodology at the back-end to manage tasks. Users can work in various modes including Scrum and Kanban. With hundreds of add-on functionalities, AI manager can quickly come up to managing an AI product Development.

Trello

Like Jeera, Trello is one of the best graphic based applications used to manage tasks and collaborate between projects and teams. It gives

10.2 AI Product Tools

outstanding flexibility and freedom to you as AI Manager to customize various project tasks including task assignment and monitoring.

ProductPlan

ProductPlan, is yet another product development roadmap management tool. This tool can be integrated with Jira and Slack as well. So, now you can exchange data between these. The roadmap so developed can be shared among the teams for better coordination and planning.

Wizeline

As a Product Manager, the process of tracking the development of the product is essential due to alterations made in data or a change in an idea. Wizeline eases the adaptation to these changes and prevents relapses in the process. The software enables feedback to be gathered from users and other stakeholders of the product. What sets Wizeline apart from other apps is the ability to analyze and codify patterns in the feedback. It converts repeated feedback into a new feature in the product's design.

UserVoice

UserVoice is product feedback gathering and analysis tool. This tool is highly effective to analyze the data that is collected as part of feedback about the product especially coming from multiple sources and then further converting them into actionable items.

Slack

Slack simply put, is the modern-day messenger in an office environment. and is extremely popular among across teams and companies. It acts as an instant communication channel enabling efficient and efficient work culture.

RescueTime

Time tracking is one of the essential elements in overall project management. While there are various tools to track the time spent on tasks related to project, invariably we also need to know how much time is being spent in various other activities overall, over a period of time. RescueTime does this by tracking time which is being spent on various activities, categorized automatically such as time spent on browsing, working on projects, and so on. This could be a great tool to assess personal productivity as well.

UXCam

UXCam or the User Experience Cam, allows you to capture even the smallest action on your app by your customer. It give you options to record, replay and hence be able to analyze the user experience. This could be used to figure-out user behavior as it is.

Zoom

This is one of the definite applications being used my managers to interact with teams and clients at geographically distant locations. So, be it voice or video calls, Zoom does it . One can also record the entire call session for future reference as well.

Balsamiq

As their website says "With Balsamiq Wireframes, anyone can design great user interfaces" is true to its words. Balsamiq allows for Prototyping, wireframing and UX ideation almost flawlessly. As an AI product manager, this is one tool you will need to share your ideas to your design team. It is a perfect application to sketch and also track changes.

Invision

Invision supports complete product design workflow stimulate in terms of productivity and creativity, while focusing on prototyping. It helps teams to collaborate and interact by showcasing and feeding back to the design.

11. Use Cases for Industries

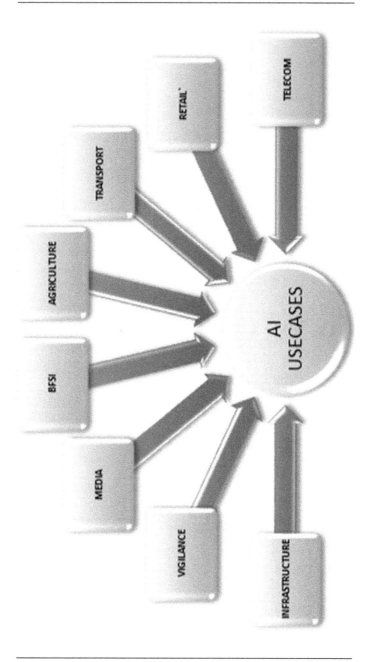

General Area

Industry Impacted: GENERAL

System/Module: VOICE BASED FOLLOW-UP MANAGER

Use Case Description: This can be used for automated command based utility that looks in for keywords and converts them into executable commands. So let's say when a speaker is speaking to a client or even if it's a general meeting or a conversation, voice-based follow-up manager picks up keywords or so from the speech and aligns them for execution.

Features/Contours:

- Improved Turn-around time
- Automatic Workflow Trigger
- Task Audit Trail

AI Model:

FACE RECOGNITION	FACE MATCH	FACE EMOTION	OCR	LIVENESS	CROWD COUNT	DROWSINESS	SENTIMENT DETECTION	SOUND ID	SPEECH ID	SPEECH CLONING	SPEECH MATCH	OBJECT DETECTION	SIGNATURE MATCH	DERMATICS	SPECTRAL IMAGING	IMAGE MAPPING	SENSORS
											X						

Industry Impacted: GENERAL

System/Module: INFRASTRUCTURE SECURITY SYSTEM

Use Case Description: This is an interesting utility. It uses various technologies including face match OCR drowsiness sentiment detection and object detection. Guard and Security Personal Monitoring System, Off Line Device Functioning such as water meter, Electricty Meters and Traffic Light Functioning indicators

Features/Contours:

- Quick Detection
- Alarming System Trigger
- Part of Integrated Security System
- Low Maintenance

AI Model:

FACE RECOGNITION	FACE MATCH	FACE EMOTION	OCR	LIVENESS	CROWD COUNT	DROWSINESS	SENTIMENT DETECTION	SOUND ID	SPEECH ID	SPEECH CLONING	SPEECH MATCH	OBJECT DETECTION	SIGNATURE MATCH	DERMATICS	SPECTRAL IMAGING	IMAGE MAPPING	SENSORS
	X		X			X	X					X					

Industry Impacted: GENERAL

System/Module: PERSONAL VIGILANCE SYSTEM

Use Case Description: Security systems like intruder detection, fencing system et cetera.

Features/Contours:

- Quick Detection

- Alarming System Trigger

- Part of Integrated Security System

- Low Maintenance

AI Model:

FACE RECOGNITION	FACE MATCH	FACE EMOTION	OCR	LIVENESS	CROWD COUNT	DROWSINESS	SENTIMENT DETECTION	SOUND ID	SPEECH ID	SPEECH CLONING	SPEECH MATCH	OBJECT DETECTION	SIGNATURE MATCH	DERMATICS	SPECTRAL IMAGING	IMAGE MAPPING	SENSORS
	X			X			X				X		X				

Media & Marketing

Industry Impacted: MEDIA & MARKETING

System/Module: CONTENT CENSOR AND RATING SYSTEM

Use Case Description: Content censoring has become a major bottleneck in the field of media and broadcasting. Due to the availability of large content on different media platforms, censoring such content has become a challenge. Using content sensor and rating system, the AI platform can be used to categorise a particular image and video contents into various ratings. This can further be implemented as a browser-based utility or a server based rating system.

So imagine this, if I as a user of social networking site wish to upload an image which is against the policy of the networking website, the browser may immediately notify about the possibility of a failure to upload such an image.

Likewise this utility may also be activated from a server side, hence rating the image as "public" or "private". Clearly a new type of categorisation can be provided to the user.

Features/Contours:

- Custom Censorship Defination

- Social Network Profile Rating

- Personalised Brower Creation based on user profile

- 100% authentic User onboarding process.

AI Model:

FACE RECOGNITION	FACE MATCH	FACE EMOTION	OCR	LIVENESS	CROWD COUNT	DROWSINESS	SENTIMENT DETECTION	SOUND ID	SPEECH ID	SPEECH CLONING	SPEECH MATCH	OBJECT DETECTION	SIGNATURE MATCH	DERMATICS	SPECTRAL IMAGING	IMAGE MAPPING	SENSORS
	X			X			X							X			

Industry Impacted: MEDIA & MARKETING

System/Module: CONTENT CONFIDENCE SCALE (FAKE)

Use Case Description: Fake news nowadays has become a harsh reality, something which seems to be inevitable. With growing media and news in particular, the instances of spreading of fake news and its implications have only reason.

These type of news has the inherent power to derail even the strongest of the governments.

AI can be used to counter this problem. Using AI one can find the information and verify its authenticity. Say for instance, generally we see images being morphed and floated on Internet. These images particularly has message supporting or disrespecting a particular community's sentiments.

AI can not only find a similar picture from the Internet but can also verify the information about the picture which may include the actual news and the context in which it was published.

Features/Contours:

- Custom Content confidence scale creation for various social domains.

- News DNA explorer.

AI Model:

FACE RECOGNITION	FACE MATCH	FACE EMOTION	OCR	LIVENESS	CROWD COUNT	DROWSINESS	SENTIMENT DETECTION	SOUND ID	SPEECH ID	SPEECH CLONING	SPEECH MATCH	OBJECT DETECTION	SIGNATURE MATCH	DERMATICS	SPECTRAL IMAGING	IMAGE MAPPING	SENSORS
	X			X	X	X	X					X					

Industry Impacted: MEDIA & MARKETING

System/Module: PERSONALIZED MARKETING FLATFORM

Use Case Description: Personalise marketing is a new concept to a large extent. Although a lot of work has been done in this field, the effectiveness is yet to be realised. In general personal marketing or individualised marketing and subsequent sale is a long and tedious process involving various steps of identification and solution implementation.

AI can not only intuitively recognise the likes and dislikes of an individual from the media or the environment they come from, but also clearly suggest relevant products and services to them, without any manual interventions.

Features/Contours:

- Customer Profile Builder
- Intelligent Advert Selector
- Marketing Impact Analysis

AI Model:

FACE RECOGNITION	FACE MATCH	FACE EMOTION	OCR	LIVENESS	CROWD COUNT	DROWSINESS	SENTIMENT DETECTION	SOUND ID	SPEECH ID	SPEECH CLONING	SPEECH MATCH	OBJECT DETECTION	SIGNATURE MATCH	DERMATICS	SPECTRAL IMAGING	IMAGE MAPPING	SENSORS
	X						X				X						

Agro and Agriculture

Industry Impacted: AGRICULTURE

System/Module: CROP, AGRI AND FOOD PROCESSING

Use Case Description: Lot of work has been done in the field of agriculture, crop production and food processing industry. However as the population of the world is increasing there is a lot to be done in improving the yield, protecting the produce, food storage and finally distribution.

There are various ways in which AI can contribute in Agro industry. To begin with disease identification in crops, especially identifying patterns on the leaf, soil consistency, and weather forecasting.

Industry Impacted: AGRICULTURE

System/Module: SOIL TEST - PREDICTIVE ANALYTICS

Use Case Description: Using AI, the farmers can predict the future production of a crop merely by using AI apps which detects the type of soil and hence its nutritional constituency. The farmers can then make an informed decision in terms of what nutrients are missing in the soil and also what type of crop should be taken up next. In this way they need not completely depend upon soil testing agencies or any other such external agency.

Features/Contours:

- Auto Soil Card Generation.
- Crop Variety Suggestion
- Crop Yield Prediction
- Pre-Market Price Indicator

AI Model:

FACE RECOGNITION	FACE MATCH	FACE EMOTION	OCR	LIVENESS	CROWD COUNT	DROWSINESS	SENTIMENT DETECTION	SOUND ID	SPEECH ID	SPEECH CLONING	SPEECH MATCH	OBJECT DETECTION	SIGNATURE MATCH	DERMATICS	SPECTRAL IMAGING	IMAGE MAPPING	SENSORS
															X	X	

Industry Impacted: AGRICULTURE

System/Module: CROP READINESS/MONITORING

Use Case Description: Readiness of a crop can be detected by an AI App. This micro-app can be a part of an entire aggro unified platform. Further the readiness of the crop can be a metric towards preparation of storage areas, building markets, and other such supporting activities in a more precise and orchestrated manner. Further, as a part of crop safety as well as yield protection, AI can be used to ensure any damage control. Using AI-based imagery, farmers can quickly identify challenging situations like fire for instance.

Features/Contours:

1. Sell Yield Plan

2. Operations Requirement

3. Logistics Management

AI Model:

FACE RECOGNITION	FACE MATCH	FACE EMOTION	OCR	LIVENESS	CROWD COUNT	DROWSINESS	SENTIMENT DETECTION	SOUND ID	SPEECH ID	SPEECH CLONING	SPEECH MATCH	OBJECT DETECTION	SIGNATURE MATCH	DERMATICS	SPECTRAL IMAGING	IMAGE MAPPING	SENSORS
																X	

Industry Impacted: AGRICULTURE

System/Module: CROP HEALTH ANALYSIS

Use Case Description: Crop gradation on the basis of yield quality can be achieved using AI apps. Again using image-based AI models a farmer can assess the quality of one's production which in turn can be used to calculate total earnings. Needless to say such apps also expedite the process of marketing and sales.

Features/Contours:

- Yield Quality Analysis

- Cropwise Custom Yield Grading

AI Model:

FACE RECOGNITION	FACE MATCH	FACE EMOTION	OCR	LIVENESS	CROWD COUNT	DROWSINESS	SENTIMENT DETECTION	SOUND ID	SPEECH ID	SPEECH CLONING	SPEECH MATCH	OBJECT DETECTION	SIGNATURE MATCH	DERMATICS	SPECTRAL IMAGING	IMAGE MAPPING	SENSORS
															X	X	

Industry Impacted: AGRICULTURE

System/Module: RAW FOOD MATERIAL QUALITY DETECTION

Use Case Description: We all love when it's fresh and probably that's the reason why most of us love to go to vegetable markets whenever we can . But raw food material quality detection is indeed a very big challenge and we as consumers completely rely upon marketing agencies and middlemen. Farmers on the other hand have no definite mechanism to claim the freshness of the of the yield. AI can help identify the freshness of food material by its colour, shape and other features.

Features/Contours:

- Market Place Product Quality Detection

AI Model:

FACE RECOGNITION	FACE MATCH	FACE EMOTION	OCR	LIVENESS	CROWD COUNT	DROWSINESS	SENTIMENT DETECTION	SOUND ID	SPEECH ID	SPEECH CLONING	SPEECH MATCH	OBJECT DETECTION	SIGNATURE MATCH	DERMATICS	SPECTRAL IMAGING	IMAGE MAPPING	SENSORS
															X	X	

Industry Impacted: AGRICULTURE

System/Module: IRRIGATION AUTOMATION PLAN

Use Case Description: Water being one of the precious resources available to human is also something that has ever been least regarded. Infact, one of the biggest reasons economies around the world to be dependent and independent has entirely relied on the fact that how much water resources are available for disposal. Adequate water irrigation facilities can be managed up using AI-based applications. Sprinklers for instance maybe started by examining the colour of the soil and not merely as a matter of timetable. Using AI apps farmers can now save a lot in terms of both power consumption and money.

Features/Contours:

- Optimize crop inputs
- Input benefit analysis at individual and co-operative level

AI Model:

FACE RECOGNITION	FACE MATCH	FACE EMOTION	OCR	LIVENESS	CROWD COUNT	DROWSINESS	SENTIMENT DETECTION	SOUND ID	SPEECH ID	SPEECH CLONING	SPEECH MATCH	OBJECT DETECTION	SIGNATURE MATCH	DERMATICS	SPECTRAL IMAGING	IMAGE MAPPING	SENSORS
																X	

Industry Impacted: PEST MANAGEMENT

System/Module: PEST RISK ASSESSMENT

Use Case Description: While talking about irrigation, one cannot ignore the effect of pests on both crop and the yield. The infestation of pests is both biological and environmental. Examining the constituents of air, pressure levels and moisture, AI can easily predict both the type and the level of pest risks.

Features/Contours:

- Prediction of Pest Attack

- Impact Analysis

- Integrated Warning Mechanism

AI Model:

FACE RECOGNITION	FACE MATCH	FACE EMOTION	OCR	LIVENESS	CROWD COUNT	DROWSINESS	SENTIMENT DETECTION	SOUND ID	SPEECH ID	SPEECH CLONING	SPEECH MATCH	OBJECT DETECTION	SIGNATURE MATCH	DERMATICS	SPECTRAL IMAGING	IMAGE MAPPING	SENSORS
																X	

Industry Impacted: LIVESTOCK

System/Module: LIVESTOCK DISEASE PREDICTION

Use Case Description: In many parts of the world a majority of agriculture is still based upon older methods of cultivation. This includes usage of cattle for various agricultural activities. However, lack of general information along with no medical assistance for these animals readily available, farmers generally tend to lose these resources. AI apps can specifically be used for detecting these diseases within the animals such as cows, ox, goats to predict their diseases and empower the farmers to a very large extent.

Features/Contours:

- Early livestock disease outbreak detection.

- Ready medical consultation availablity from an enpanelled Vet.

- Part of Integrated Animal Diseases Detection and Prevention Platform

- Readily available medical reports.

- Local Disease Pattern prediction

AI Model:

FACE RECOGNITION	FACE MATCH	FACE EMOTION	OCR	LIVENESS	CROWD COUNT	DROWSINESS	SENTIMENT DETECTION	SOUND ID	SPEECH ID	SPEECH CLONING	SPEECH MATCH	OBJECT DETECTION	SIGNATURE MATCH	DERMATICS	SPECTRAL IMAGING	IMAGE MAPPING	SENSORS
														X		X	

Industry Impacted: AGRICULTURE

System/Module: YIELD PREDICTION

Use Case Description: Although farmers understand their crop yields, still many of them still struggle with the future yield that they are going to reap. Imagine a situation where a farmer is able to calculate the future yield based on the current situation of the field. One can now not only plan to market and sell his produce readily, but also contribute towards the overall agricultural ecosystem in terms of both demand and supply.

Features/Contours:

- Yield Estimation
- Designer Yield
- Loan and Budget Plan
- Part of Integrated Unified Agro Platform

BFSI

Industry Impacted: BANKING, FINANCE, INSURANCE

System/Module: FRAUD PREVENTION

Use Case Description: Checking of financial instruments, bank checks for instance, takes away a lot of significant time financial institutions put in. For instance verifying signatures on a bank cheque is a time-consuming activity. Using AI-based systems, this process can be automated. This will have a direct positive impact on the productivity and the turnaround time of bank services.

Features/Contours:

Customer Profiling

- N no. instruments processing per minute
- Efficiency & Productivity improvement

AI Model:

FACE RECOGNITION	FACE MATCH	FACE EMOTION	OCR	LIVENESS	CROWD COUNT	DROWSINESS	SENTIMENT DETECTION	SOUND ID	SPEECH ID	SPEECH CLONING	SPEECH MATCH	OBJECT DETECTION	SIGNATURE MATCH	DERMATICS	SPECTRAL IMAGING	IMAGE MAPPING	SENSORS
	X		X	X									X				

Industry Impacted: BANKING, FINANCE, INSURANCE

System/Module: CREDIT APPROVAL PROCESS IMPROVEMENT

Use Case Description: Traditionally credit disbursement has been the main motive behind banking. However, as one progressed into the future, we see that credit approvals take a lot of time and effort. Intelligent applications can take care of this by analysing the overall client portfolio from various sources including credit rating, banking systems, insurance and overall client social background.

Features/Contours:

- Reduced Turnaround Time (TAT) for Credit Approval
- Client 360 degree Credit Rating

AI Model:

FACE RECOGNITION	FACE MATCH	FACE EMOTION	OCR	LIVENESS	CROWD COUNT	DROWSINESS	SENTIMENT DETECTION	SOUND ID	SPEECH ID	SPEECH CLONING	SPEECH MATCH	OBJECT DETECTION	SIGNATURE MATCH	DERMATICS	SPECTRAL IMAGING	IMAGE MAPPING	SENSORS
		X											X			X	

Industry Impacted: BANKING, FINANCE, INSURANCE

System/Module: CLIENT PORTFOLIO ASSESSMENT

Use Case Description: AI crawlers can be used to a certain the portfolio of a client. This can be done by analysing various financial aspects of a customer including overall bank balance, credit card payment defaults, expenditure pattern and overall defaults from various websites.

Features/Contours:

- Authentic Client Profiling
- Reduced Forgery

AI Model:

FACE RECOGNITION	FACE MATCH	FACE EMOTION	OCR	LIVENESS	CROWD COUNT	DROWSINESS	SENTIMENT DETECTION	SOUND ID	SPEECH ID	SPEECH CLONING	SPEECH MATCH	OBJECT DETECTION	SIGNATURE MATCH	DERMATICS	SPECTRAL IMAGING	IMAGE MAPPING	SENSORS
	X		X										X			X	

HRM

Industry Impacted: BANKING, FINANCE, INSURANCE

System/Module: ATTENDENCE MAINTENANCE

Use Case Description: Face ID-based recognition system can not only help manage the day-to-day attendance maintenance problem but can also improve the overall productivity of HR. Automatic reports about an employee's presence in the office can also be generated with these AI applications. These apps can detect "last seen"status of an employee, for instance. Some of the other advantages include, Efficient Attendence Logging, Authentic attendence and hence no proxy solution, reduced waiting time to log, low maintenance cost soultion, and impression free.

Features/Contours:

- Quicker on-boarding.

- Impressionless attendence marking.

- Reduction in time taken to log in.

AI Model:

FACE RECOGNITION	FACE MATCH	FACE EMOTION	OCR	LIVENESS	CROWD COUNT	DROWSINESS	SENTIMENT DETECTION	SOUND ID	SPEECH ID	SPEECH CLONING	SPEECH MATCH	OBJECT DETECTION	SIGNATURE MATCH	DERMATICS	SPECTRAL IMAGING	IMAGE MAPPING	SENSORS
	X			X	X												

Authentication & Security

Industry Impacted: BANKING, FINANCE, INSURANCE

System/Module: VOICE BASED USER AUTHENTICATION

Use Case Description: Use of NLP in customer verification and identification process in banking and other such can greatly enhance the security of such systems. Unli ke in most banking systems where a customer is identified by the customer ID, a new verification technique can be implemented using voice and face match. This can further be assisted by the liveliness feature of AI apps.

Models can be implemented to eliminate any intrusion possibilities including checking for fake image-voice pair. This would also improve the turnaround time as it would decrease the waiting time for customers to get through the system.

Parallelly, the module can be used as a biometric authencation solution,. This would be difficult to spoof and much easier to use. Both Text dependent and Text independent methods may be implemented for speaker recognisation.

Features/Contours:

1. Neutral Accent enabled.

2. Multi-language support.

3. Local Verinaculars Support

4. Efficient and Powerful integration with CRM

AI Model:

FACE RECOGNITION	FACE MATCH	FACE EMOTION	OCR	LIVENESS	CROWD COUNT	DROWSINESS	SENTIMENT DETECTION	SOUND ID	SPEECH ID	SPEECH CLONING	SPEECH MATCH	OBJECT DETECTION	SIGNATURE MATCH	DERMATICS	SPECTRAL IMAGING	IMAGE MAPPING	SENSORS
											X						

Insurance

Industry Impacted: BANKING, FINANCE, INSURANCE

System/Module: CLAIM PROCESSING

Use Case Description: AI-based OCR models can do wonders in processing claims automatically. Instead of checking the forms manually, these apps can extract keyvalue pairs from the form and authenticate them against the system. These can give further impressive results as in most cases the claims are submitted electronically. Hence, verification and extraction of data from valid IDs such as passports, driving licences can be achieved through this.

Features/Contours:

- Authentic Client Profiling
- Reduced Forgery
- Faster Transcription
- Error-free/Reduced Error Production
- Integration with workflow management tools
- Improved document search capability

AI Model:

FACE RECOGNITION	FACE MATCH	FACE EMOTION	OCR	LIVENESS	CROWD COUNT	DROWSINESS	SENTIMENT DETECTION	SOUND ID	SPEECH ID	SPEECH CLONING	SPEECH MATCH	OBJECT DETECTION	SIGNATURE MATCH	DERMATICS	SPECTRAL IMAGING	IMAGE MAPPING	SENSORS
	X		X	X							X		X			X	

Transport & Traffic Management

Industry Impacted: TRANSPORT

System/Module: TRANSPORT

Use Case Description: Transportation is one of the most promising areas where AI can deliver. There are various areas where AI can solve some of the most pressing issues

Industry Impacted: TRANSPORT

System/Module: TRAFFIC MANAGEMENT

Use Case Description: Using aerial photography captured by drones as well as static images picked up from roadside streetlights can be used to identify bottlenecks and other traffic issues on the road. For instance a wrongly parked vehicle can be a source of traffic congestion or problem with a vehicle can pose a jam such issues can be easily identified by AI modules using image processing and heat maps. Traffic management is a macro umbrella under which other sub systems may function making it an unified platform.

Features/Contours:

- Information processing to predict incidents.

- Auto accident detection and signalling system

- Traffic congestion prediction

- Appropriate Traffic Strategiy Suggestion.

- Direct communication with the Vehicle.

- Vehicle Profiling

AI Model:

FACE RECOGNITION	FACE MATCH	FACE EMOTION	OCR	LIVENESS	CROWD COUNT	DROWSINESS	SENTIMENT DETECTION	SOUND ID	SPEECH ID	SPEECH CLONING	SPEECH MATCH	OBJECT DETECTION	SIGNATURE MATCH	DERMATICS	SPECTRAL IMAGING	IMAGE MAPPING	SENSORS
	X				X						X	X			X	X	

Industry Impacted: TRANSPORT

System/Module: TARRIF MANAGEMENT

Use Case Description: Toll collection is one of the biggest revenue sources for any government. However absence of intelligent tariff management forces commuters to pay unjustified fee, at the same time government and administration have no means to consolidate their collection efforts leading to setting up of huge infrastructure including manpower at the tolls. Using AI models customised tarrif management solutions can be implemented wherein vehicle category may be identified and relevant tariff may be charged. For instance there may be different tariff for cars and a separate fee for commercial trucks. AI models may include object identification.

Features/Contours:

- Custom Tarrif generation based upon vehicle type

Auto Drives

Industry Impacted: TRANSPORT

System/Module: AUTO DRIVES

Use Case Description: Auto driving has always facinated humans for a very log time. Although, I'm not a huge fan of auto driving but still unsupported the sheer fact that it provides a lot of convenience. Imagine a taxi appears in front of your gate within seconds of your request from your app. There have been attempts by engineers and scientists to implement this technology on full-scale however, the complexities involved in its implementation has always rattled them. To drives this, combination of multiple AI technologies including image mapping, sensory, IOT devices, NLP-based solutions and more such shall be needed.

One of the best implementations of auto drives could be in a regulated environment. College campus for instance could be a great scenario where such a technology can be implemented. Others may include highways, private estates, gated complexes.

Features/Contours:

- Part of integrated Urban Transport Infrastructure

- Efficient & Safe Transport system

- Co-ordinated Transport

- Easy Fleet Management

- Safe, Secure and convenient

Industry Impacted: TRANSPORT

System/Module: PASSENGER SECURITY SYSTEM

Use Case Description: AI-based passenger security systems may well be implemented wherein auto check-ins can be performed by the system. This can be done using face match, voice match, and liveliness tests. One can also implement other features like total passenger count, passenger monitoring and passenger surveillance. Say for instance in an airport the exact location of the passenger or customers entering into the premises can precisely be tracked using face match and cam locations.

It will not only help identify a person in the premises with their exact position but also deters antisocial elements.

Features/Contours:

- Passenger Profiling
- Passengers Count
- Custom Survelliance

Industry Impacted: TRANSPORT

System/Module: DRIVER MONITORING SOLUTION

Use Case Description: Driver monitoring system is a fabulous idea which is both implementable as well as beneficial. A large number of accidents on the roads happen because the driver has been driving for hours and dozed off for split seconds. And this is the time when accidents occur. Driver monitoring system can precisely scan and subsequently alert the driver from sleeping. Using drowsiness feature, the software can quickly alert the user from sleeping. In fact an entire ecosystem can be built around this feature specially for a transportation company where goods are being transported from one place to another on long-distance.

Features/Contours:

- Driver Alertness Profile
- Traffic Vigilance
- Driver Alert System
- Intruder Detection

AI Model:

FACE RECOGNITION	FACE MATCH	FACE EMOTION	OCR	LIVENESS	CROWD COUNT	DROWSINESS	SENTIMENT DETECTION	SOUND ID	SPEECH ID	SPEECH CLONING	SPEECH MATCH	OBJECT DETECTION	SIGNATURE MATCH	DERMATICS	SPECTRAL IMAGING	IMAGE MAPPING	SENSORS
	X				X	X					X	X				X	

Supplies Management

Industry Impacted: TRANSPORT

System/Module: AUTO PART REORDERING

Use Case Description: Spare parts and auto parts retail sector heavily depends upon the demand and the supply from its customers. A large number of such customers rely on local malls and shops. Such large shops need a lot of staff to ensure parts are available and do not go below the required quantity from the display areas. Using rack images clicked by the in-house cameras, AI apps can quickly determine the quantity that needs to be reordered.

Features/Contours:

- Automatic Stock Replacement Alert

- Instant Theft instane capture and alert

AI Model:

FACE RECOGNITION	FACE MATCH	FACE EMOTION	OCR	LIVENESS	CROWD COUNT	DROWSINESS	SENTIMENT DETECTION	SOUND ID	SPEECH ID	SPEECH CLONING	SPEECH MATCH	OBJECT DETECTION	SIGNATURE MATCH	DERMATICS	SPECTRAL IMAGING	IMAGE MAPPING	SENSORS
		X														X	

Industry Impacted: TRANSPORT

System/Module: NEAREST - PARKING LOT FINDER

Use Case Description: We all have struggled to find the nearest parking lot whenever we have entered into one. And for most of us, it has been frustrating to find out that there was one available closest to the exit gate when we had parked our vehicles far off. And this is precisely what parking lot Finder does. This can be easily be achieved with pre-marked signs on the parking space. AI app can easily detect both the number of parking lots available as well as the location of these lots. Once the driver gets his parking ticket, it may include the parking lot number as an. Alternatively an SMS may also be sent on his mobile with this information.

Features/Contours:

- Vehicle Entry Alert

- Empty Lot finder

- Lot Intrusion Detection

- Better Space Management

Retail

Industry Impacted: RETAIL

System/Module: CASHLESS MONEY

Use Case Description: Face money can be introduced for conducting money transfers in retail sector. Hence you no more need to carry wallets or cash. With certain security features including anti-spoofing, secondary authentication for transaction approval, cashless money is the thing of present and the future. You go to a store to buy your favourite bread, and check-in into an AI app either at the counter or various locations in the store. You show your face and some gesture to confirm the transaction. The money from your wallet automatically is transferred to the retailer.

Features/Contours:

- Swift Wallet Money transfer
- Authorised Money
- Restrictive Money/Capping Facility
- Convenient and easy

AI Model:

FACE RECOGNITION	FACE MATCH	FACE EMOTION	OCR	LIVENESS	CROWD COUNT	DROWSINESS	SENTIMENT DETECTION	SOUND ID	SPEECH ID	SPEECH CLONING	SPEECH MATCH	OBJECT DETECTION	SIGNATURE MATCH	DERMATICS	SPECTRAL IMAGING	IMAGE MAPPING	SENSORS
	X		X				X				X		X			X	

Industry Impacted: RETAIL

System/Module: FOOTFALL ANALYSIS

Use Case Description: For this is very important in placesFootfall, it is the total number of people entering into a premises. Places where large gathering such as public meetings areas and malls exists, need footfall analysis to be undertaken. AI in this regard can do wonders. Footfall analysis can precisely calculate the number of people entering into a premises. It can also provide gender-based reports such as the total children present, aged, males and females.

Features/Contours:

- Crowd Management

- Safety Augmentation Alert

- Demographic/Gender based alerts

AI Model:

FACE RECOGNITION	FACE MATCH	FACE EMOTION	OCR	LIVENESS	CROWD COUNT	DROWSINESS	SENTIMENT DETECTION	SOUND ID	SPEECH ID	SPEECH CLONING	SPEECH MATCH	OBJECT DETECTION	SIGNATURE MATCH	DERMATICS	SPECTRAL IMAGING	IMAGE MAPPING	SENSORS
	X				X										X		

Telecom & Mobile

Industry Impacted: MOBILE & TELECOM

System/Module: PERSONAL ASSISTANTS

Use Case Description: Various types of personalised assistance can be developed using AI. Siri for instance is one such example. However, in this case, customised personal assistants can be developed. Imagine this scenario where one is able to unlock a mobile phone using voice commands.

Features/Contours:

- Personalisation Voice Training
- Create Voice Commands

AI Model:

FACE RECOGNITION	FACE MATCH	FACE EMOTION	OCR	LIVENESS	CROWD COUNT	DROWSINESS	SENTIMENT DETECTION	SOUND ID	SPEECH ID	SPEECH CLONING	SPEECH MATCH	OBJECT DETECTION	SIGNATURE MATCH	DERMATICS	SPECTRAL IMAGING	IMAGE MAPPING	SENSORS
	X			X			X				X					X	

Spamming

Industry Impacted: MOBILE & TELECOM

System/Module: SMS - ANTI-SPAM SOLUTION

Use Case Description: Nowadays as we understand we receive a lot of spam both on email as well as on mobiles. Email system can be developed and trained further to identify spam SMS. With this app one can block all SMSes which are likely to be spam.

Features/Contours:

- Fast detection

- Low Cost Solution

AI Model:

FACE RECOGNITION	FACE MATCH	FACE EMOTION	OCR	LIVENESS	CROWD COUNT	DROWSINESS	SENTIMENT DETECTION	SOUND ID	SPEECH ID	SPEECH CLONING	SPEECH MATCH	OBJECT DETECTION	SIGNATURE MATCH	DERMATICS	SPECTRAL IMAGING	IMAGE MAPPING	SENSORS
			X				X										

Education & Training

Industry Impacted: EDUCATION & TRAINING

System/Module: PERSONALIZED LEARNING

Use Case Description: Personalised learning is a huge opportunity for AI implementation. One of the best use cases is using an AI app that one can generate a psychometric profile of a student. This profile can further be used to identify both the motivation as well as the need to train a student. This profile can also be generated using various psychometric tests or based on DMIT techniques. For instance if a child is introvert training can be imparted using various non-activity based techniques and vice versa.

Features/Contours:

- Student psychometric profile generation
- Custom training material mapping
- Student learning progress report

AI Model:

FACE RECOGNITION	FACE MATCH	FACE EMOTION	OCR	LIVENESS	CROWD COUNT	DROWSINESS	SENTIMENT DETECTION	SOUND ID	SPEECH ID	SPEECH CLONING	SPEECH MATCH	OBJECT DETECTION	SIGNATURE MATCH	DERMATICS	SPECTRAL IMAGING	IMAGE MAPPING	SENSORS
	X		X				X				X	X				X	

Industry Impacted: EDUCATION & TRAINING

System/Module: GRADE AUTOMATION

Use Case Description: Grades for the written work using AI-based grade automation. Written work for instance can be marked using AI

Features/Contours:

- Vector and Raster input support

- Grammar check

- Overall sentiment check

- Grade card generation

AI Model:

FACE RECOGNITION	FACE MATCH	FACE EMOTION	OCR	LIVENESS	CROWD COUNT	DROWSINESS	SENTIMENT DETECTION	SOUND ID	SPEECH ID	SPEECH CLONING	SPEECH MATCH	OBJECT DETECTION	SIGNATURE MATCH	DERMATICS	SPECTRAL IMAGING	IMAGE MAPPING	SENSORS
			X									X				X	

Industry Impacted: EDUCATION & TRAINING

System/Module: ADAPTIVE LEARNING

Use Case Description: Adaptive learning is a systematic process of understanding the pedagogy behind once learning and then adapting itself to the same. So for instance, if a student is assigned a default path of learning, based on his past performance, AI application and plan over or in other words reroute the learning objectives.

Features/Contours:

- Student Learning pattern generation
- Realtime adaptive training material
- Student learning progress report

AI Model:

FACE RECOGNITION	FACE MATCH	FACE EMOTION	OCR	LIVENESS	CROWD COUNT	DROWSINESS	SENTIMENT DETECTION	SOUND ID	SPEECH ID	SPEECH CLONING	SPEECH MATCH	OBJECT DETECTION	SIGNATURE MATCH	DERMATICS	SPECTRAL IMAGING	IMAGE MAPPING	SENSORS
	X						X				X					X	

Psychometry

Industry Impacted: EDUCATION & TRAINING

System/Module: PSYCHOMETRIC ANAYLSIS - GENERAL/DMIT

Use Case Description: DMIT had been in the industry for quite sometime now. A lot of work has been done in this field. From a personality perspective understanding one's nature, attitude, preferences has become easier using Dermatoglyphics Multiple Intelligence Test (DMIT). Using fingerprint analysis at the core and imaging as the AI counterpart, psychometric analysis report can be generated.

Features/Contours:

- DMIT candidate profile
- Offline report Generation

AI Model:

FACE RECOGNITION	FACE MATCH	FACE EMOTION	OCR	LIVENESS	CROWD COUNT	DROWSINESS	SENTIMENT DETECTION	SOUND ID	SPEECH ID	SPEECH CLONING	SPEECH MATCH	OBJECT DETECTION	SIGNATURE MATCH	DERMATICS	SPECTRAL IMAGING	IMAGE MAPPING	SENSORS
	X														X		X	

171

Office Automation

Industry Impacted: COMMUNICATION

System/Module: MOM MANAGER

Use Case Description: MOM or minutes of meeting is indeed a pain in the neck for many. Writing down all the aspects of a meeting can be both tiresome and complex needless to mention it as an unproductive work. To get away with this as AI app can be developed which converts speech into text and then emails the same to all the participants of the meeting.

Features/Contours:

- Tasks - Todo list generator
- Workflow manager
- Auto task assignment
- Customer request true audit trail

AI Model:

FACE RECOGNITION	FACE MATCH	FACE EMOTION	OCR	LIVENESS	CROWD COUNT	DROWSINESS	SENTIMENT DETECTION	SOUND ID	SPEECH ID	SPEECH CLONING	SPEECH MATCH	OBJECT DETECTION	SIGNATURE MATCH	DERMATICS	SPECTRAL IMAGING	IMAGE MAPPING	SENSORS
	X						X				X					X	

Industry Impacted: COMMUNICATION

System/Module: SEARCHABLE VOICE FILES

Use Case Description: Searching voice files is comparatively a new and revolutionary idea. There is both a requirement and opportunity in this field today using AI one can not only collect music but also catalogue the same which further can be used to search music. Likewise, lectures can also be digitised into searchable voice files. This will make accessing information both faster and convenient.

Features/Contours:

- Custom cataloging

- Indexing and annotation

AI Model:

FACE RECOGNITION	FACE MATCH	FACE EMOTION	OCR	LIVENESS	CROWD COUNT	DROWSINESS	SENTIMENT DETECTION	SOUND ID	SPEECH ID	SPEECH CLONING	SPEECH MATCH	OBJECT DETECTION	SIGNATURE MATCH	DERMATICS	SPECTRAL IMAGING	IMAGE MAPPING	SENSORS
							X				X						

Voice Processing

Industry Impacted: COMMUNICATION

System/Module: EMOTION ANALYSER

Use Case Description: Primarily emotions are captured in real life by looking at the people. However, people whom one cannot interact face-to-face it becomes challenging to understand. Emotion analyser can precisely detect the tone of the speakers and react to the situation accordingly. This can also be used to summarise emotions and pickup the right keywords.

Features/Contours:

- Mood predictor
- Task generator
- Part of Omni-channel Customer Support platform

AI Model:

FACE RECOGNITION	FACE MATCH	FACE EMOTION	OCR	LIVENESS	CROWD COUNT	DROWSINESS	SENTIMENT DETECTION	SOUND ID	SPEECH ID	SPEECH CLONING	SPEECH MATCH	OBJECT DETECTION	SIGNATURE MATCH	DERMATICS	SPECTRAL IMAGING	IMAGE MAPPING	SENSORS
	X						X				X						

Industry Impacted: CALL CENTER

System/Module: CONVERSATION CAPTURE

Use Case Description: This is an absolute practical application for a call center. All the conversation between the agent and the customers can be captured and converted into text. For future processing. Also, using the text summerization, a brief summar may be produced.

Features/Contours:

- Conversation logger
- Transcript Generator
- Customer Experience (CX) Audit trail
- Interaction Summary Generator

AI Model:

FACE RECOGNITION	FACE MATCH	FACE EMOTION	OCR	LIVENESS	CROWD COUNT	DROWSINESS	SENTIMENT DETECTION	SOUND ID	SPEECH ID	SPEECH CLONING	SPEECH MATCH	OBJECT DETECTION	SIGNATURE MATCH	DERMATICS	SPECTRAL IMAGING	IMAGE MAPPING	SENSORS
											X						

Industry Impacted: CALL CENTER

System/Module: SENTIMENT ANALYSER

Use Case Description: There is a huge need to analyse the feedback of the customers. However, it is equally difficult process to get the same from the customer. While many outrightly deny, other don't give their true feedback. Analysing one's sentiments can be produced. Using AI, the final call result may be labelled as "Satisfied", "Dissatisfied" etc.

Features/Contours:

- True "Happy" Customer" Analyser
- Feedback Rubric Generator
- Repeat business Predictor

AI Model:

FACE RECOGNITION	FACE MATCH	FACE EMOTION	OCR	LIVENESS	CROWD COUNT	DROWSINESS	SENTIMENT DETECTION	SOUND ID	SPEECH ID	SPEECH CLONING	SPEECH MATCH	OBJECT DETECTION	SIGNATURE MATCH	DERMATICS	SPECTRAL IMAGING	IMAGE MAPPING	SENSORS
							X				X						

Industry Impacted: CALL CENTER

System/Module: VOICE BASED USER AUTH.

Use Case Description: While call centers have brought-in a revolution in the field of customer service, over a period time clearly, waiting to be served on call is frustrating. One of the ways to reduce this wait time could be reducing the customer authentication process. Using Voice recongnition, this time lag may be reduced.

Features/Contours:

- Neutral Accent enabled.
- Multi-language support.
- Local Verinaculars Support
- Efficient and Powerful integration with CRM

AI Model:

FACE RECOGNITION	FACE MATCH	FACE EMOTION	OCR	LIVENESS	CROWD COUNT	DROWSINESS	SENTIMENT DETECTION	SOUND ID	SPEECH ID	SPEECH CLONING	SPEECH MATCH	OBJECT DETECTION	SIGNATURE MATCH	DERMATICS	SPECTRAL IMAGING	IMAGE MAPPING	SENSORS
											X						

Industry Impacted: CALL CENTER

System/Module: VOICE BASED CUSTOMER FEEDBACK

Use Case Description: NLP or natural language processing can be implemented to first record and then dictate the feedback into the system. So a set of feedback questions may be asked to the customers and let them respond verbally.

Features/Contours:

- Personalised Feedback Generator

- Customer Feedback Auto analyser

AI Model:

FACE RECOGNITION	FACE MATCH	FACE EMOTION	OCR	LIVENESS	CROWD COUNT	DROWSINESS	SENTIMENT DETECTION	SOUND ID	SPEECH ID	SPEECH CLONING	SPEECH MATCH	OBJECT DETECTION	SIGNATURE MATCH	DERMATICS	SPECTRAL IMAGING	IMAGE MAPPING	SENSORS
											X						

Industry Impacted: CALL CENTER

System/Module: ANTI-SPAM SOLUTION - EMAIL

Use Case Description: Email Spam is a huge problem both for corporates as well individuals. With training on spam content, AI system can be designed to filter such emails.

Features/Contours:

- Pattern based Anti-spamming solution

AI Model:

FACE RECOGNITION	FACE MATCH	FACE EMOTION	OCR	LIVENESS	CROWD COUNT	DROWSINESS	SENTIMENT DETECTION	SOUND ID	SPEECH ID	SPEECH CLONING	SPEECH MATCH	OBJECT DETECTION	SIGNATURE MATCH	DERMATICS	SPECTRAL IMAGING	IMAGE MAPPING	SENSORS
			X													X	

Customer Service & Hospitality

Industry Impacted: HOSPITALITY

System/Module: SMART ROOMS

Use Case Description: House Construction with uber cool technology features is the thing of the hour. Ranging from home security, intruder detaction to enhancement such as voice-controlled Home lighting, AI-based Smart homes can be designed.

Features/Contours:

- Voice based ambiance control
- temperature ccontrol
- electricty management

AI Model:

FACE RECOGNITION	FACE MATCH	FACE EMOTION	OCR	LIVENESS	CROWD COUNT	DROWSINESS	SENTIMENT DETECTION	SOUND ID	SPEECH ID	SPEECH CLONING	SPEECH MATCH	OBJECT DETECTION	SIGNATURE MATCH	DERMATICS	SPECTRAL IMAGING	IMAGE MAPPING	SENSORS
	X	X		X	X		X				X					X	

Industry Impacted: HOSPITALITY

System/Module: HOBOTS - CS

Use Case Description: "HOBOTS" or Hospatility Robots are already being used at various hotels. Such Hobots are installed at the recieption to assist customers and clients with their desk requests. These NLP based AI-Bots converse with customers by understanding what they speak and responding appropriately.

Features/Contours:

- Multi-Language support
- 24X7 support
- Personalised Concerige Services
- Real-time Recommendations

AI Model:

FACE RECOGNITION	FACE MATCH	FACE EMOTION	OCR	LIVENESS	CROWD COUNT	DROWSINESS	SENTIMENT DETECTION	SOUND ID	SPEECH ID	SPEECH CLONING	SPEECH MATCH	OBJECT DETECTION	SIGNATURE MATCH	DERMATICS	SPECTRAL IMAGING	IMAGE MAPPING	SENSORS
X	X		X	X			X	X	X	X	X		X			X	

Medical Care

Industry Impacted: MEDICAL & HEALTHCARE

System/Module: IMAGE BASED PRE-DIAGNOSTICS

Use Case Description: Medical imaging as a part of patient diagnostics is a huge area of implementation for AI based solutions. Various AI-application based on medical imagery such as X-ray, MRI, CT-Scan and Ultrasound can be developed for early diagnoses of lung cancer, various forms of repiratory diseases, bone deformation, dental problems, retina related issues including glaucoma, tumors, Alzheimer and more.

Features/Contours:

- Multi-disease prediction
- Smart and Convienent
- Remotly Accessible

AI Model:

FACE RECOGNITION	FACE MATCH	FACE EMOTION	OCR	LIVENESS	CROWD COUNT	DROWSINESS	SENTIMENT DETECTION	SOUND ID	SPEECH ID	SPEECH CLONING	SPEECH MATCH	OBJECT DETECTION	SIGNATURE MATCH	DERMATICS	SPECTRAL IMAGING	IMAGE MAPPING	SENSORS
X	X													X	X	X	

Industry Impacted: MEDICAL & HEALTHCARE

System/Module: CASHLESS SETTLEMENT

Use Case Description: Imagine you go to a store, buy some stuff and just pay by showing your face. Cashless Settlement is the thing of the future. One can quickly pay by various mechanism.

Features/Contours:

- Multi-Currency Support

AI Model:

FACE RECOGNITION	FACE MATCH	FACE EMOTION	OCR	LIVENESS	CROWD COUNT	DROWSINESS	SENTIMENT DETECTION	SOUND ID	SPEECH ID	SPEECH CLONING	SPEECH MATCH	OBJECT DETECTION	SIGNATURE MATCH	DERMATICS	SPECTRAL IMAGING	IMAGE MAPPING	SENSORS
X	X	X		X							X						

Industry Impacted: MEDICAL & HEALTHCARE

System/Module: SONAR PRE-DIAGNOSTICS

Use Case Description: Noninvasive medical test reports generated using sound can be analysed to pre-diagnose diseases. As a matter of fact, direct sound files generated through the machines such as ultra sound or the echo may also be used to perform the same.

Features/Contours:

- Multi-disease prediction
- Smart and Convienent
- Remotly Accessible

AI Model:

FACE RECOGNITION	FACE MATCH	FACE EMOTION	OCR	LIVENESS	CROWD COUNT	DROWSINESS	SENTIMENT DETECTION	SOUND ID	SPEECH ID	SPEECH CLONING	SPEECH MATCH	OBJECT DETECTION	SIGNATURE MATCH	DERMATICS	SPECTRAL IMAGING	IMAGE MAPPING	SENSORS
X	X							X	X								

Industry Impacted: MEDICAL & HEALTHCARE

System/Module: EPIDEMIC PREDICTION

Use Case Description: Some of the epidemics may be predicted convincingly by analysing various parameters including percentage moisture in the air, bacterial levels, and various seasonal elements such as likelihood of rain and so on.

Features/Contours:

- Early warning system

- Various types of epidemic detection

AI Model:

FACE RECOGNITION	FACE MATCH	FACE EMOTION	OCR	LIVENESS	CROWD COUNT	DROWSINESS	SENTIMENT DETECTION	SOUND ID	SPEECH ID	SPEECH CLONING	SPEECH MATCH	OBJECT DETECTION	SIGNATURE MATCH	DERMATICS	SPECTRAL IMAGING	IMAGE MAPPING	SENSORS
X																X	X

Industry Impacted: MEDICAL & HEALTHCARE

System/Module: GENOME

Use Case Description: Although mostly the human genome remains the same for all of us. However, a negligible yet crucial percentage is responsible for the difference in both appearance and health among us. AI-based analysis of various genome graphs may help predict various diseases that may onset in one's future. Alzimer, diabetes and other such can be convincingly predicted with this.

Features/Contours:

- Multi-disease early prediction
- Trusted Predictions for serious diseases

Industry Impacted: DEFENCE

System/Module: ANTI-DRONE SYSTEM

Use Case Description: Drone detection, enemy vehicle detection using object detection and OCR & OMR, any vehicular movement and much more can captured using highend imaging, thermal maps and frequency mapping. This can further be augmented with sonar and radio feed to create an entire air field. Further such systems may directly be co-ordinated and attached with missile system to make it a true automated defence system.

Features/Contours:

1. Real-time drone detection classification and warning system

2. High Precision based

3. Multi sensor detection and verification

AI Model:

FACE RECOGNITION	FACE MATCH	FACE EMOTION	OCR	LIVENESS	CROWD COUNT	DROWSINESS	SENTIMENT DETECTION	SOUND ID	SPEECH ID	SPEECH CLONING	SPEECH MATCH	OBJECT DETECTION	SIGNATURE MATCH	DERMATICS	SPECTRAL IMAGING	IMAGE MAPPING	SENSORS
					X							X			X	X	X

Defense

Industry Impacted: DEFENCE

System/Module: UNAUTHORIZED ACTIVITY
DETECTION

Use Case Description: Images captured from the video feed may be used to identify any unauthorised activity. These can then be integrated with the alarm system or any defence system. So imagine cameras detect some movement in an area. Using the Object detection, AI module can detect the object and classify the same as "danger" or "safe" and accordingly trigger series of actions.

Features/Contours:

- Day-Night support

- Intelligent agents

AI Model:

FACE RECOGNITION	FACE MATCH	FACE EMOTION	OCR	LIVENESS	CROWD COUNT	DROWSINESS	SENTIMENT DETECTION	SOUND ID	SPEECH ID	SPEECH CLONING	SPEECH MATCH	OBJECT DETECTION	SIGNATURE MATCH	DERMATICS	SPECTRAL IMAGING	IMAGE MAPPING	SENSORS
X	X	X			X							X				X	

Home Lifestyle

Industry Impacted: HOME SOLUTION

System/Module: PERSONAL ASSISTANTS

Use Case Description: Imagine a home where everything is voice enabled. Voice commands can be used for various purposes including opening Parking lots, Garrages, Entry systems and more of such.

Features/Contours:

- Secure, Convinent, Low Maintenance

AI Model:

FACE RECOGNITION	FACE MATCH	FACE EMOTION	OCR	LIVENESS	CROWD COUNT	DROWSINESS	SENTIMENT DETECTION	SOUND ID	SPEECH ID	SPEECH CLONING	SPEECH MATCH	OBJECT DETECTION	SIGNATURE MATCH	DERMATICS	SPECTRAL IMAGING	IMAGE MAPPING	SENSORS
X	X	X						X		X						X	X

Industry Impacted: HOME SOLUTION

System/Module: AMBIANCE CONTROL

Use Case Description: Lot of tasks could be undertakenjust by speaking. One can control Home Lighting, temperature control and such by simply speaking to listening device,

Features/Contours:

- Voice based ambiance control
- temperature ccontrol
- electricty management

AI Model:

FACE RECOGNITION	FACE MATCH	FACE EMOTION	OCR	LIVENESS	CROWD COUNT	DROWSINESS	SENTIMENT DETECTION	SOUND ID	SPEECH ID	SPEECH CLONING	SPEECH MATCH	OBJECT DETECTION	SIGNATURE MATCH	DERMATICS	SPECTRAL IMAGING	IMAGE MAPPING	SENSORS
X	X				X	X			X			X				X	X

Testing & Durability

Industry Impacted: CONSTRUCTION

System/Module: MATERIAL TESTING - NDT

Use Case Description: NDT (Non-destructive Testing) is a common testing undertaken in various industries such as Linear Utility, Shipping, and other such industries where metals such as Iron, Steel and like are required to be tested for various quality parameters. For instance, a quality of wield, depth of paint, level of rust and on.

Features/Contours:

- Usage in various metal industries

- Fast, convienent and low cost Testing solution

AI Model:

FACE RECOGNITION	FACE MATCH	FACE EMOTION	OCR	LIVENESS	CROWD COUNT	DROWSINESS	SENTIMENT DETECTION	SOUND ID	SPEECH ID	SPEECH CLONING	SPEECH MATCH	OBJECT DETECTION	SIGNATURE MATCH	DERMATICS	SPECTRAL IMAGING	IMAGE MAPPING	SENSORS
								X				X			X	X	

Entertainment

Industry Impacted: MUSIC & ENTERTAINMENT

System/Module: PERSONALIZED AVATARS

Use Case Description: Create personal avators, which can then be used to represent oneself in various softwares. Another place where avatars can be implemented is at chatbots. Imagine a customised avatar with a realistic customer support.

Features/Contours:

- Designer avatars

- Custom behaviour

AI Model:

FACE RECOGNITION	FACE MATCH	FACE EMOTION	OCR	LIVENESS	CROWD COUNT	DROWSINESS	SENTIMENT DETECTION	SOUND ID	SPEECH ID	SPEECH CLONING	SPEECH MATCH	OBJECT DETECTION	SIGNATURE MATCH	DERMATICS	SPECTRAL IMAGING	IMAGE MAPPING	SENSORS
X	X	X		X					X		X					X	

Industry Impacted: MUSIC & ENTERTAINMENT

System/Module: MUSIC RECOMMENDATION

Use Case Description: AI app can recommend music based on one's mood, place and expression on one's face. So picture this. You start from your office in the evening. Your app detects your face and plays a certain music. Likewise, you are out for shopping and AI module autoatically starts playing certain music.

Features/Contours:

- Easy Music curation

AI Model:

FACE RECOGNITION	FACE MATCH	FACE EMOTION	OCR	LIVENESS	CROWD COUNT	DROWSINESS	SENTIMENT DETECTION	SOUND ID	SPEECH ID	SPEECH CLONING	SPEECH MATCH	OBJECT DETECTION	SIGNATURE MATCH	DERMATICS	SPECTRAL IMAGING	IMAGE MAPPING	SENSORS
	X	X					X	X									

Industry Impacted: MUSIC & ENTERTAINMENT

System/Module: AUDIO CLASSIFICATION

Use Case Description: Now-a-days, everyone has audio libraries on their mobiles. And this is a big problem. It takes a lot of time to classify music. AI can categorise music based on music genre.

Features/Contours:

- Convinent Sorting and seeking capability
- Easy Copyright
- Easy Notes Generation

AI Model:

FACE RECOGNITION	FACE MATCH	FACE EMOTION	OCR	LIVENESS	CROWD COUNT	DROWSINESS	SENTIMENT DETECTION	SOUND ID	SPEECH ID	SPEECH CLONING	SPEECH MATCH	OBJECT DETECTION	SIGNATURE MATCH	DERMATICS	SPECTRAL IMAGING	IMAGE MAPPING	SENSORS
							X	X									

Industry Impacted: MUSIC & ENTERTAINMENT

System/Module: MUSIC TRANSCRIPTION

Use Case Description: Further, music can be cataloged according to the lyrics. This will help in searching the music quicker. Since, this could be a herculian task, AI module can extract lyrics and other details as need be and generate an index, based on which music search can be performed.

Features/Contours:

- Convinent Sorting and seeking capability
- Easy Copyright
- Easy Notes Generation

AI Model:

FACE RECOGNITION	FACE MATCH	FACE EMOTION	OCR	LIVENESS	CROWD COUNT	DROWSINESS	SENTIMENT DETECTION	SOUND ID	SPEECH ID	SPEECH CLONING	SPEECH MATCH	OBJECT DETECTION	SIGNATURE MATCH	DERMATICS	SPECTRAL IMAGING	IMAGE MAPPING	SENSORS
							X	X	X		X						

Fashion

Industry Impacted: FASHION DESIGNING & TECHNOLOGY

System/Module: AI-BASED CUSTOM DESIGN PRODUCTION

Use Case Description: This AI module could be both interesting & extremely helpful for those designers who struggle to suggest the best possible designs before finalizing them. AI can quickly recommend designs based upon certain preferences. For example one's own personality, color, music, food, clothes and so on. AI module can predict the kind of designs a customer may shortlist based upon the above mentioned metrics and fasten the process of design selection

Features/Contours:

- Personalised Design Creation
- Improved TAT, Finalization time

AI Model:

FACE RECOGNITION	FACE MATCH	FACE EMOTION	OCR	LIVENESS	CROWD COUNT	DROWSINESS	SENTIMENT DETECTION	SOUND ID	SPEECH ID	SPEECH CLONING	SPEECH MATCH	OBJECT DETECTION	SIGNATURE MATCH	DERMATICS	SPECTRAL IMAGING	IMAGE MAPPING	SENSORS
	X												X	X		X	

12. Finally

Now that we have pushed ourselves to knowing more about this new found "Final Frontier" called AI, the question is "what next?".

While some of the concepts in AI can be overwhelming for people coming from a non-technical background, the ideal clearly has been to introduce the reader to various facets of this domain. As someone coming from a non-technical background with years of experience in managing business and product development, my first advice would be to ascertain your interest area within the AI domain. While one can always choose to work as a Data Scientist, the skill of an individual, one's interest and most importantly the appitude for the same will matter the most.

Having said this, I recommend a three-step process to induce yourself into AI.

One, it would be a great idea to start spending more time in understanding how AI can help your own industry or the domain you work in. Look around to analyze how AI can impact your daily work, how it can benefit your colleagues, the process they work in, and finally the business. So, not only looking for AI new use cases, but also being creative in this will help you to start sailing. One may start imagining new use cases for various spheres of work. This initiative will automatically force you to the next step.

The next step would need you to work more in-depth into this field. As you start finding more use cases, the subsequent logical question would be how to implement AI in these use cases. And when I say this I mean, technically. By now you have enough fodder to chew upon in terms of what to do. By now one can also expect to pick and choose one area of interest in AI to work upon. Be it computer vision or NLP and start reading through various articles and journals about various AI models (API) available in that area. By going through the models that various players in the industry have developed, will provide a lot of clarity in terms of implementing the same.

And finally now that you have enough understanding of how AI works in terms of use cases and various AI algorithms available that can be used to implement in use cases, you now have an option to actually go ahead and implement the same hands-on.

For this clearly, you will need to have the technical skills. Since, Python is being extensively used for AI development, it would be a great idea to start learning it first before venturing into other software products and tools. Simultaneously, I would strongly recommend you to build up your skills in both Mathematics and Statistics. This would immensely help in strengthening your AI programming capabilities in general.

In furtherance, although the lack of understanding of certain topics in these subjects may pose to be deterrent in getting into the core AI, one may choose to just appreciate this technology and only work from a management perspective hence by allowing one not to actually work on AI as a technology resource.

In all, AI is bound to touch every aspect of current and the future generations to come. We may choose to avoid it, but can never ignore it.

Opportunities are knocking at our doors and we must not slumber.